Abba Hillel Silver and American Zionism

Edited by

MARK A. RAIDER
State University of New York

JONATHAN D. SARNA
Brandeis University

and RONALD W. ZWEIG
Tel Aviv University

FRANK CASS
LONDON • PORTLAND, OR

First published in 1977 in Great Britain by
FRANK CASS PUBLISHERS
Newbury House, 900 Eastern Avenue
London IG2 7HH

and in the United States of America by
FRANK CASS PUBLISHERS
c/o ISBS, 5804 N.E. Hassalo Street
Portland, Oregon 97213-3644

Website: http://www.frankcass.com

Library of Congress Cataloging-in-Publication Data

Rabbi Abba Hillel Silver and American Zionism / edited by Mark A.
Raider, Jonathan D. Sarna, and Ronald W. Zweig.
p. cm.
Includes bibliographical references and index.
ISBN 0-7146-4824-8 (hc). – ISBN 0-7146-4377-7 (pbk.)
1. Silver, Abba Hillel, 1893–1963. 2. Rabbis–Ohio–Cleveland–
Biography. 3. Zionists–United States–biography. 4. Zionism–
United States–History. 5. Ben-Gurion, David, 1886–1973.
I. Raider, Mark A. II. Sarna, Jonathan D. III. Zweig, Ronald W.
BM755.S544Z56   1997
320.54'095694
[B]-DC21   97-26840
                                                          CIP
                                                          r97

British Library Cataloguing in Publication Data

Abba Hillel Silver and American Zionism
1. Silver, Abba Hillel – Political and social views 2. Rabbis – Biography 3. Zionism
I. Raider, Mark A. II. Sarna, Jonathan D. III. Zweig, Ronald W.
320.5'4'095694'092

ISBN 0-7146-4824-8 (cloth)
ISBN 0-7146-4377-7 (paper)

This group of studies first appeared in a Special Issue on 'Abba Hillel Silver and
American Zionism' in The Journal of Israeli History, Vol.17, No.1, Spring 1996.

Printed in Great Britain by Antony Rowe Ltd., Chippenham, Wiltshire

ABBA HILLEL SILVER AND AMERICAN ZIONISM

Contents

Introduction

In his lifetime Rabbi Abba Hillel Silver (1893–1963) was among the giants in Jewish life who labored effectively on the world stage for the creation of the State of Israel during the turbulent period preceding the birth of the modern Jewish state. He ranks with American Zionist leaders such as Louis D. Brandeis, Stephen S. Wise and Henrietta Szold, and Zionism's preeminent international figures, Theodor Herzl, Chaim Weizmann and David Ben-Gurion.

Silver's career has only recently begun to receive systematic scholarly scrutiny. The microfilm edition of the Abba Hillel Silver Papers, a treasure trove hitherto inaccessible to all but a select few, was acquired for Brandeis University through the generosity of the Lucius N. Littauer Foundation. To celebrate, Brandeis University invited distinguished scholars and students of American Jewish life and Zionism to utilize the Silver microfilm and other research materials to reexamine the life and career of this extraordinary figure. The resulting April 1996 symposium on "The Zionist Career of Rabbi Abba Hillel Silver" was inspired by Mr. Jacques Torczyner and supported by Brandeis University's Jacob and Libby Goodman Institute for the Study of Zionism and Israel and the Department of Near Eastern and Judaic Studies. The conference was also generously supported by Mr. Raphael D. Silver and family.

The essays present, for the first time, a comprehensive overview of Silver's Zionist thought, political strategy and vision. They illuminate central questions concerning Silver's distinctive contribution to the Zionist enterprise: How, for example, did his career as a rabbi inform his approach as a Zionist leader? What was the source of his political strength? What kind of impact did he have on the campaign for Jewish statehood?

The present volume seeks to demonstrate that Silver's biography holds significant implications for modern Jewish history and, in particular, the history of the Jewish national movement and the State of Israel. The centenary of political Zionism and the fiftieth anniversary of the establishment of the State of Israel make this a timely initiative. The essays, which originally appeared in a special issue of the *Journal of Israeli History*, shed new light on the path of this distinguished tribune of American Judaism and champion of Zionism.

We express special thanks to the scholars who participated in the symposium at Brandeis University for allowing us to include their papers in this volume. We are most grateful to Sylvia Fuks Fried of the Tauber Institute for the Study of European Jewry, Miriam Greenfield of the *Journal of Israeli History*, and Jonathan Manley, editor of Frank Cass, for their invaluable efforts in seeing this volume through to publication.

Mark A. Raider	Jonathan D. Sarna	Ronald W. Zweig
Albany, New York	Waltham, Massachusetts	Tel Aviv

Rosh Hodesh Iyar 5757
Spring 1997

Zionism and Judaism:
The Path of Rabbi Abba Hillel Silver

Rabbi Alexander M. Schindler

ABBA HILLEL SILVER WAS ONE OF THE GIANTS of his generation, endowed with a commanding personality, with rare oratorical talent, with a wide-ranging intellect and uncommon political skills. He was a powerfully persuasive lobbyist for Zionism in Washington and at the United Nations. In the 1930s, others may have challenged his pre-eminence; however, during the fateful 1940s, no one else on the American Jewish scene exceeded him in stature.

Unfortunately, Abba Hillel Silver's preeminence was overshadowed by subsequent events. In this he shared the fate of Stephen S. Wise, his arch-rival and that other rabbinic titan of his time. Their greatness was eclipsed by their successes. They strove to redeem the Jewish people from the genocidal crimes of Nazism by assuring the establishment of modern Israel. They succeeded gloriously, but only to be quickly replaced in the historical spotlight by the leaders of the newborn Jewish state. They sought to reorganize the American Jewish community and to mobilize its latent political power. But in this arena too they were soon replaced by federations and lay organizations that ultimately became the main wielders of American Jewish communal influence.

The stature of these rabbis and their allies among lay leaders has been diminished also by more than a few modern Jewish historians who, at best, have obscured their heroism for us by depictions of raw, rude and contentious politics in which they participated as midwives to the diplomatic birthing of Israel. At worst, American Jewish leaders of the period are portrayed as impotent, or even as criminally culpable in their inability to halt or slacken the genocidal onslaught. Indeed, some historians have charged that American Zionist leadership ignored or even sacrificed rescue efforts for the sake of building the Jewish community in Palestine and transforming the Yishuv into a state. The American Jewish Commission on the Holocaust, formed in September of 1981 with Arthur Goldberg as chair, was riven by internal dissension within the year and did little to modify this perception. Thus it was that the greatness of Silver and Wise was eclipsed, not only by their successes, but also by their perceived failures in a historical context dramatically different from our own, which, once taken into account, considerably softens the harsh judgment of their failures even as it amplifies our appreciation of their triumphs.

During the years of the Great Depression, the rise of Nazism had cast a global penumbra of anti-Semitism. In the late 1930s an American Jewish Committee study found that more than one-third of Americans believed that Jews were "too powerful." This proportion actually grew to a majority during the war. More than sixty per cent of all Americans at the time believed that the "persecution of Jews in Europe had been their own fault." And of this hostile sector, twenty per cent said that they would "drive Jews out of the United States" naming them as a "menace to America," not unlike the Germans and the Japanese who resided in America. American Jews and their leadership faced an environment bristling with anti-Semitic organizations and rabble rousers, such as the German-American Bund, the Silver Shirts, Father Coughlin, Gerald L.K. Smith, and the American aviator hero Charles Lindbergh. Discrimination against Jews consistently revealed itself in housing, employment and education. Add to this a thirty per cent unemployment rate, and an anti-immigration fervor that resulted in the introduction of 60 anti-immigration bills in the year 1939 alone. So extreme was opposition to immigration that in a survey taken that year, more than two-thirds of the American public opposed a one-time exception to quota limits that would have allowed 10,000 refugee children to enter the United States.

Conceivably a true mass movement in favor of rescue might have moved President Franklin D. Roosevelt to override the Congress, the State Department, the War Department and all the many other forces which obstinately opposed the opening of America's shut doors. But the Jewish community was helplessly isolated in a hostile environment, with few, if any, allies, receiving no support from the trade union movement (of which Rabbi Silver, it should be noted, was a champion, resigning from Cleveland's Chamber of Commerce in 1921 to protest its open-shop policies). There was no active civil rights movement to mobilize, nor any of the many other liberal alliances that have been key to Jewish advancement in the postwar era. Moreover, the genocidal reality of Nazi anti-Semitism had loomed up too suddenly out of the historical continuum. It was too unprecedented, even given our martyrology spanning the millennia. It was too much of a horror, a crime before God, to be fully grasped.

Searching the horizon for even a glimmer of light, Abba Hillel Silver found hope and purpose in the possibility of establishing a Jewish national presence in Palestine. This conviction that had been forged in his youth was hardened by the revelation that Europe had become a killing field for Jews. The fulfillment of the Zionist vision, said Silver, was the

> inescapable logic of events....From the infested, typhus-ridden Ghetto of Warsaw, from the death-block of Nazi occupied lands, where millions of our

people are awaiting execution by the slow or the quick method, from a hundred concentration camps which befoul the map of Europe, over the entire face of the earth, comes the cry: "enough; there must be a final end to all this, a sure and certain end."[1]

First among the obstacles to that "sure and certain end" was the British White Paper of 1939, which limited Jewish immigration to 75,000 over five years. It was a policy that squeezed Jews into Hitler's death trap. Yet at the 21st World Zionist Congress in Geneva, Chaim Weizmann advocated a policy of cautious compromise with Great Britain in order to preserve unity against the Nazis. Abba Hillel Silver, in one of his first appearances on the World Zionist scene, spoke in support of Weizmann's approach.

But this was the last time that Silver would advocate Zionist dependency upon the powers-that-be. He thundered: "The tragic problems of the Jewish people in the world cannot be solved by chiefs of government or prominent officials sending us Rosh Hashanah greetings!"[2] Silver quickly became a dynamo of militant Zionism. Within three years he would electrify the Biltmore Conference with a historic speech urging and winning — under the leadership of Ben-Gurion — an unequivocal demand for the establishment of a Jewish commonwealth in Palestine. By 1943, he had full control of the Emergency Committee for Zionist Affairs and turned it into a powerhouse for lobbying and agitation.

Silver's strategy was to mobilize the Jewish rank-and-file and to build widespread popular support for the Zionist cause. Distrustful of the Roosevelt administration, he insisted on political independence for himself and for Zionism. He registered as a Republican, but supported candidates of both major parties for public office. This militant, self-assertive strategy brought Silver into a head-on collision with Nahum Goldmann and with Stephen Wise, who advocated using channels of influence that he himself had established during forty years of public service and Zionist activism. Their furious factional fights have been the object of retrospective criticism, but our judgment must be leavened by the historical context. During much of the prewar period, Zionism was still a minority movement rejected by mainstream Jews of every stripe as too "ideological." Silver's own Central Conference of American Rabbis was on the record as anti-Zionist, at least de jure though not de facto, until 1937.

Likewise were the Conservative and Orthodox streams of Judaism, including virtually all the Hasidic dynasties, opposed to what they regarded

1   Marc Lee Raphael, Abba Hillel Silver: A Profile in American Judaism, New York, 1989.
2   Ibid.

as a pseudo-Messianic, dangerously secular pipe dream. The influential American Jewish Committee was also vigorously opposed to Zionism. So was the Jewish Left; socialists and communists both preferred other political destinies for the Jewish people. History overruled them all, as the Zionist cause was pushed to the fore, morally and politically, in the name of Jewish survival. It was too late, Silver argued,

> to wage anew those interesting ideological battles of a generation ago...the vast ghostly company [of murdered Jews] give us no rest...it is their innocent blood which will not be covered up, until out of their martyrdom a new life is born the free and redeemed life of their people.[3]

In their Zionism, Stephen S. Wise and Abba Hillel Silver were united. Perhaps it would be more accurate to view their rivalry as a functional partnership. Together, they hitched their dream to the great draft horse America. Silver, the militant, swept Great Britain and other obstacles out of her path. Wise, the diplomat, fed and groomed the beast, thereby helping non-Zionist Jews to hop onto the wagon. Eventually, the mighty horse did its labor. Then other Jewish leaders took over the reins.

Rabbi Silver's role within the movement of Reform Judaism assuredly was a dominant and recurrent theme of his life's work. Reform was still anti-Zionist during the early years of Silver's career. And even during his mid-years — when he had many kindred spirits in the rabbinic Conference — the leaders of the Central Conference of American Rabbis (CCAR) and the Hebrew Union College were steadfast in their conviction, as articulated by Plank Five of the radical 1885 Pittsburgh Platform, that Jews are "not a nation but a religious community and therefore expect no return to Palestine." Certainly the predominant majority of Reform's lay men and women at that time were of such a mind. They were still captive of Reform's past, of its revolutionary period of anti-Orthodox rationalism and rejectionism. They affirmed, rather, that Reform is a missionary, "universal" faith, fundamentally incompatible with national aspirations. Silver remained impervious to the anti-Zionism within the Reform movement and indelibly impressed his Zionist faith upon the movement as a whole. The process took three decades, and many played a role, not least the almost three million Eastern European Jews who immigrated to the US between 1881 and 1920. These new immigrants defined their Jewishness in ethnic rather than in universal terms. They sensed themselves to be a "national minority," a

---

3   Ibid.

people within peoples — and once their sons entered the Reform rabbinate, as did the Lithuanian-born Silver, the balance of power within the movement began to shift. The Eastern European Jews moved away from the strictures of Orthodoxy, and Reform moved away from its rather cold intellectualism born in the Age of Reason. These mutually reinforcing developments served to pave the road to Reform's acceptance of Zionism.

Abba Hillel Silver gave elegant voice to these historical forces. He did so most effectively in a 1935 debate with the venerated Rabbi Samuel Schulman before the Central Conference of American Rabbis. Their subject, the anti-Zionist Fifth Plank of the Pittsburgh Platform, still stood, *de jure*, as the mission statement of Reform. "It is idle," said Silver,

> to talk of our people as no longer a nation but a religious community, in the face of the fact that millions of Jews are today recognized by the law of nations as national minorities, (in many Eastern European countries) millions more as a distinct nationality in Soviet Russia, and hundreds of thousands in Palestine where a Jewish homeland is being created under the terms of a mandate of the League of Nations which recognizes not only the national existence of the Jewish people, but also its historic claim to a national home.[4]

Silver did not reject the messianic universalism or missionary purpose of Reform. He only refused to see either as a substitute for Jewish nationalism. Rather, he urged "the sense of classic harmony in Jewish life, the total program of Jewish life and destiny...the religious and moral values, the universal concepts, the concept of mission, as well as the Jewish people itself."[5] This was indeed the Zionism of the Eastern European immigrants, the folk from whom the Lithuanian-born Silver drew his personal and political strength. Most of them would never immigrate to Israel, even as Silver; but all of them would come to see Israel as their spiritual homeland, the main repository of Jewish values and the main preserver of their Jewish identities. In their breadth of understanding about the meaning of Judaism and Jewish peoplehood in the modern world, Schulman and Silver did not stand at polar opposites. Silver did not uphold the strict secular nationalism that was dominant in Palestine, but rather affirmed a "spiritual Zionism," thus retaining Classical Reform's commitments to the concept of Israel's world-wide mission. And Schulman, on his part, was no exponent of a pure, undiluted Classical Reform. Indeed, in his passionate presentation, he acknowledged Reform's excessive "self-satisfied rationalistic pride" and called

4   1935 *Yearbook of Central Conference of American Rabbis.*
5   Ibid.

for greater Jewish distinctiveness and ritual observances in the movement.[6] Still, the two by virtue of their age, descent and demeanor, represented the opposing tendencies within Reform Judaism: the one, a noble conservatism that feared Zionism's potential to diminish permanently the prophetic, universal character of Judaism, the other, a militant realism that viewed the flesh-and-blood fact of Jewish suffering as alterable only through a restoration of Jewish nationhood.

At its 1937 conference in Columbus, Ohio, the CCAR adopted the Guiding Principles. Plank Five now declared Judaism to be "the soul of which Israel is the body." And it went on to affirm "the rehabilitation of Palestine, the land hallowed by memories and hopes," as a "center of Jewish culture and spiritual life." The declaration was hardly Zionist. It carefully declared Palestine to be *a* center, not *the* center. But it ended the isolation of Reform Judaism from the mainstream of American Jews who were, in large part under Silver's leadership, becoming increasingly devoted to Jewish efforts in Palestine. As the Columbus debate came to its conclusion, Rabbi David Philipson, who fifty years before had attended the convocation adopting the Pittsburgh Platform, declared: "If the younger men of the Central Conference want this revision, I will move its adoption."[7] In truth, that task had been performed two years earlier, and even 20 years earlier, by Abba Hillel Silver.

Just as he spoke within the Reform movement as a Zionist, so did Abba Hillel Silver speak within the Zionist movement as a rabbi. Silver's only English biographer, Marc Raphael, portrayed his protagonist as a Zionist, first and foremost, judging his rabbinic vocation only of subordinate weight. He considered Silver a cultural rather than a religious Zionist.[8] Not so! Abba Hillel Silver was a deeply religious Jew. As a teacher and preacher, he was committed to the synagogue as the central institution of Jewish life, and to Judaism as the bedrock of Jewish life. In a 1948 address delivered at a Union of American Hebrew Congregations (UAHC) Assembly, he declared:

> There are no substitutes in Jewish life for religion. Neither philanthropy nor culture nor nationalism is adequate for the stress and challenge of our lives. All these interests can and must find their rightful place within the general pattern of Judaism. But the pattern must be of Judaism, the Judaism of the priest, the prophet, the saint, the mystic and the rabbi; the Judaism which speaks of God and the worship of God, and the commandments of God and the quest for God.[9]

6   Ibid.
7   *1937 Yearbook of Central Conference of American Rabbis.*
8   Raphael, *Silver.*
9   Proceedings of the 1948 Biennial Assembly of the UAHC.

Silver did not assert these views to the members of a synagogue movement only. He spoke in like manner to the Zionists, infusing their movement with religious fervor, even as he advocated the centrality of religion in the larger Jewish community. Thus, in the mid-1920s, when the *Menorah Journal*, the most influential publication of its day, ran a series of articles highly critical of organized Judaism and belittling religion "as but a small part of the total fullness of Jewish life,"[10] Silver launched an angry counter-attack. "Why do the heathen rage?" He roared, defending the modern rabbinate and the synagogue against those intellectuals who sought to supplant religious institutions with secular alternatives. He insisted that Reform Judaism's concept of mission alone could prompt Jews to global action.[11] This holistic, religiously rooted sense of Jewish life became the hallmark of Reform Judaism in the postwar years, as it took on the challenge of being both broad and deep, flexible and rooted, as a modern religious movement. For Abba Hillel Silver, such an approach was the hallmark of his career. His famed eloquence was augmented, no doubt, by his charisma, his penetrating basso voice, his height and stature, even his bushy hair reaching to the heavens. But most of all, it was the product of his religious depth, of his fiery faith.

Silver literally steeped himself in the Torah, the prophets and the Biblical writings, so much so that biblical passages became an integral part of his internal vocabulary and pattern of communication. He didn't merely cite verses in his speeches; the Torah spoke through him. He wasn't merely rabbinical in his political style; his politics arose from his identity as a rabbi. In the schismatic world in which Abba Hillel Silver wielded his tremendous influence, he was often regarded as ruthless and militant, an avid polemicist, a general who thrived on the battlefield and defined his compatriots in reductionist terms, either as valued allies or as implacable foes. Perhaps this was a reaction to his patrician manner, his evident pride, his impermeable privacy. But perhaps too, there is among his detractors an element of "murmuring against Moses," the Biblical figure to whom Rabbi Silver bore striking resemblance and about whom he wrote in his last published book.[12]

Like Moses, he was revered more than loved as a leader aloof from the people, yet embodying their most precious hopes. Like Moses, he undertook a multiplicity of roles that demanded incredible endurance and spiritual discipline. Like Moses, he helped make tangible the dream of land for the people of Israel, and then surrendered the mantle of leadership to practical men — to administrators and warriors. And like the great liberator and

10 Raphael, *Silver*.
11 Ibid.
12 Ibid.

teacher of the Torah, Abba Hillel Silver possessed a panoramic, inclusive vision of Judaism and the Jewish people that was unique among his more nearsighted Zionist contemporaries. While the theories and plans of others were being swept away by the storm winds of history that so radically altered the Jewish landscape of our time, Silver stood upon the rock of 35 centuries of Jewish reality and saw through the tempest to the future. He wrote in his most enduring book, *Where Judaism Differed*:

> There is clearly visible in Judaism, a steady and dominant coherence, a self-consistency, which links together all its stages of change and development and gives it structure and unity of tone and character. It possesses a unity not of a system, but of a symphony — unity, freedom, and compassion — came to be sufficiently distinctive and impressive as to be unmistakable.[13]

---

13 Abba Hillel Silver, *Where Judaism Differed: An Inquiry into the Distinctiveness of Judaism*, Philadelphia, 1957, pp. 6-7.

Abba Hillel Silver as Zionist
within the Camp of Reform Judaism

Michael A. Meyer

IN HIS ADULATORY HEBREW BIOGRAPHY of Abba Hillel Silver, Isaiah Vinograd wrote: "In Silver's heart the idea took shape to conquer Reform Judaism for the Zionist idea and through it to impose the idea of the [Jewish national] renaissance upon all of America."[1] It was with this purpose in mind that Silver became associated with the Reform movement. If he could conquer the most powerful and resistant citadel of anti-Zionism, all opposition to Silver's fundamental ideology of Zionism would melt away. Vinograd's implication is clear: Silver was always a Zionist at heart; his allegiance to Reform Judaism was, above all, a tactic to serve the Zionist cause.

This view that Silver's loyalties lay fundamentally with Zionism is echoed, though less blatantly, by Marc Lee Raphael in the only full-length biography of Silver in English.

> Silver was primarily a Zionist for whom Jewish statehood and Hebrew culture were increasingly the highest values of his career, and for whom the constant use of Hebrew demonstrated the importance he attached to cultural Zionism throughout his life. He was above all else a Zionist, albeit of the American kind.

According to Raphael, this distinguishes Silver from men like Stephen S. Wise, James Heller and Louis Newman, whom he identifies as "Reform rabbis who were Zionists."[2]

The views of Vinograd and Raphael differ sharply from those of other writers on Silver, specifically of men who knew him personally within the Reform movement as well as within Zionist circles. Herbert Weiner called the rabbinate "the central commitment of Abba Hillel Silver's life."[3] David

---

1   Isaiah Vinograd, *Abba Hillel Silver: Life, Vision, Achievement* (Hebrew), Tel Aviv, 1957, p. 61.
2   Marc Lee Raphael, *Abba Hillel Silver: A Profile in American Judaism*, New York and London, 1989, p. 215.
3   Herbert Weiner, ed., *Therefore Choose Life: Selected Sermons, Addresses, and Writings of Abba Hillel Silver*, vol. 1, Cleveland and New York, 1967, p. vii.

Polish cites this passage in Weiner and adds, perhaps in intended contradiction to Vinograd's view: "Silver believed in the compatibility of Reform and Zionism, not the conquest of Reform by Zionism. For him, Zionism represented a vital addition to Reform, not a substitute."[4] Similarly, his close friend — though not, like him, a confirmed Zionist — Solomon Freehof claimed of Silver that "the rabbinate was central to his heart and mind," that "Rabbi Silver was the title which he cherished most" and that "wherever he spoke, at whatever great Jewish assemblage, or in the councils of the nations, he spoke as a Rabbi."[5]

There is a measure of truth in each of these opposing views. Surely, Silver was interested in winning over the Jewish religious establishment for Zionism. The most blatant admission of this motive of which I am aware occurs in a letter to fellow Zionist Reform rabbi James G. Heller of Cincinnati. In 1929, Stephen S. Wise had proposed organizing Reform and Conservative Zionist rabbis to formulate a united program of liberal religion and Zionism. Heller supported this project and proposed it to Silver, who responded disdainfully: "I believe it is poor tactics to say the least. Our objective should be not to divide the American rabbinate into two sharply distinguished and opposite groups, but in winning control over all existing Rabbinical organizations for Zionist purposes."[6] But Silver also insisted that his achievements as a Zionist were "never separate or apart from my profession as a rabbi. Zionism was always a part of my conception of historic Judaism, and I came to it not as a secular nationalist but as a devout Jew."[7]

Clearly the matter is complex: one of dual loyalties, sometimes in severe conflict with one another. Silver felt not fully at home in a Reform Judaism that was not Zionist, but was just as unhappy in a Zionism that espoused secular nationalism. He was, I believe, a deeply religious Zionist, whose religion was, ironically perhaps, Classical Reform Judaism. That Classical Reform Judaism at the beginning of Silver's career was dominantly, if not wholly, anti-Zionist. He certainly did seek to "Zionize" it, but to do so from the position of his own Reform commitment. Beginning with his student days at the Hebrew Union College, he was always — in sharp contrast to Stephen S. Wise — a *ben bayit* (one of its own) within the movement. His

---

4   David Polish, *Renew Our Days: The Zionist Issue in Reform Judaism*, Jerusalem, 1976, p. 117.
5   Solomon Freehof, "Abba Hillel Silver," *Central Conference of American Rabbis Yearbook* (hereafter CCARY), vol. 74, 1964, p. 159.
6   Abba Hillel Silver to James G. Heller, December 23, 1930, The Papers of Abba Hillel Silver (Papers), Western Reserve Historical Society, Cleveland, Ohio, Roll 18, Folder 387. Cf. Leon I. Feuer, "The Influence of Abba Hillel Silver on the Evolution of Reform Judaism," in Jack Bemporad, ed., *A Rational Faith: Essays in Honor of Levi A. Olan*, New York, 1977, p. 81.
7   CCARY, vol. 73, 1963, p. 163.

struggles to make Reform Judaism over in his own image were fought from within, not as one conquers a foreign citadel but as a dispute among members of the same family. This article will trace the various stages of that dispute focusing on the crucial arguments and actions in relation to the development of the movement and to Silver's rabbinical and Zionist careers.

The Hebrew Union College

When Silver came to Cincinnati in 1911, the Hebrew Union College was still recovering from the dispute between anti-Zionists and Zionists that had contributed to the departure of three faculty members a few years earlier. The Reform theologian Kaufmann Kohler remained president of the institution but, Silver recalls, students were free to preach their senior sermons on Zionist topics if they chose to do so. There was no ideological indoctrination. Kohler had appointed David Neumark, a close associate of Ahad Ha-Am, as professor of philosophy, and it was under his aegis that a Hebrew-speaking society was organized among the students. Although the Reform movement continued to be dominated by German Jews, candidates for the rabbinate were increasingly coming from the ranks of East European Jewry.

Still, the Jewish atmosphere was quite different from what the young Silver had experienced in Lithuania and New York. Given the traditional character of his parental home, it remains a bit strange that he should have chosen Hebrew Union College over the Jewish Theological Seminary. Silver himself explained it in religious terms: "I and my young friends were reaching out, quite unconsciously, for a more liberal type of Judaism."[8] He recalled that his awareness of Reform Zionists such as Gustav Gottheil, Judah Magnes, and Stephen Wise, played a role in his decision.

Clearly Silver was quite content in Cincinnati, where he founded a student magazine and gave the valedictory address. And the experience transformed him. He emerged after four years as a Classical Reform Jew, fully dedicated to a non-halakhic Judaism that stressed, above all, the message of the Prophets and the ethical mission of Israel.[9]

---

8 Autobiography/memoirs, Papers, 211/1, p. 5A.
9 His boyhood friend and lifelong associate in Zionist affairs, Emanuel Neumann, saw the transformation as entirely external: "The years passed and a new Silver emerged, whom we did not easily identify with the boy we had known. Elegant in dress, polished in manner, faultless in speech, he appeared to have undergone a transformation. He had shed the habits and manners, the accents of his earlier environment. He seemed 'goyish.' It all smacked of 'assimilation.' " Neumann did not recognize that a deeper transformation had taken place. Emanuel Neumann, *Abba Hillel Silver: Militant Zionist*, New York, 1967, p. 6.

Silver always remained a loyal alumnus of the Hebrew Union College. He served a term as president of its Alumni Association and as a member of its Board of Governors; he delivered addresses for Founders' Day and Ordination; and he sent his son there for a rabbinical education. In 1925 he received an earned doctoral degree from the College; he was himself a generous donor to its campaigns and helped to raise funds for it in Cleveland. Silver claimed to have sent more students to the College than any other rabbi. During the 1930s a group of students in Cincinnati prided themselves on being his disciples.[10] In 1947 the non-Zionist rabbi Edgar Magnin even proposed that Silver should become president of the Hebrew Union College, a suggestion Silver declined because he thought the College should be led by "a person far less controversial than I am."[11]

Of course, Silver's loyalty to the College was dependent on its maintaining at least a neutral attitude toward Zionism. When he heard that the anti-Zionist rabbi Louis Wolsey questioned a prospective student he had sponsored during his admission interview regarding his Zionism and impressed upon him its incompatibility with Reform Judaism, Silver fired off an angry letter to the registrar stating that if anti-Zionism has become a requisite, "I should like to be informed, so that I may be guided in my relation to the institution in the future." The registrar reassured Silver that, in fact, not only was this student admitted by unanimous vote, but the College had no policy with regard to the Zionism or non-Zionism of its student body.[12]

Silver's relations with Kaufmann Kohler's successor as president of the Hebrew Union College, Julian Morgenstern, had their distinct ups and downs. Morgenstern greatly appreciated and wanted to preserve Silver's loyalty to the College, the more so as the other great Zionist Liberal rabbi, Stephen S. Wise, headed a rival seminary. He offered Silver an honorary degree in 1941, attributing its award to recognition of his recent service as president of the United Palestine Appeal.[13] But he was not a political Zionist. When Silver, as President of the Alumni Association, urged that the association join in sponsoring a National Conference for Palestine to meet with the visiting Chaim Weizmann in 1937, Morgenstern was hesitant and expressed misgivings, especially as the planned conference might affiliate itself with the American Jewish Congress, headed by Wise. "On the other hand," he noted, "we owe that courtesy [to at least be present] to Weitzmann [sic] and doubly so since Weitzmann himself, as the holder of an honorary

10 George Lieberman to Silver, November 17, 1935, Papers 193/99.
11 Silver to Edgar F. Magnin, February 12, 1947, Papers, 29/678.
12 Henry Englander to Silver, September 11, 1924, Papers, 28/665.
13 Julian Morgenstern to Silver, January 23, 1941, Papers, 29/675.

degree from the Hebrew Union College, is actually an honorary member of our alumni association."[14]

In the early 1940s, however, relations between Morgenstern and Silver became severely strained. Morgenstern not only joined the "non-Zionist" American Council for Judaism but, with limited success, attempted to persuade his faculty to sign on as well. In his opening-day address to the student body in the fall of 1943, he declared Revisionist Zionism "practically identical with Nazist and Fascist theory." (It was reported in the press as referring to Zionism *tout court*.)[15] Silver now turned on Morgenstern, with whom he had even until then maintained cordial relations,[16] and supported Rabbi Joshua Loth Liebman's public protest, justifying his action because he believed the address had hurt the College. Deluged by letters and telegrams of protest, Silver was prepared to go even further than Liebman and bring charges against Morgenstern to the board of the College.[17] Clearly, Silver perceived the statement as most unfortunate and perhaps reacted as strongly as he did because it served to embarrass him in Zionist circles.[18] With Morgenstern's eventual, if lukewarm, conversion to political Zionism following the war and the new presidency of Nelson Glueck, Silver renewed his close association with the College, which lasted to the end of his life.

The Young Star of Reform Judaism

With remarkable rapidity the newly ordained Abba Hillel Silver rose to the top of the Reform movement. After barely two years in Wheeling, West Virginia, — at the age of twenty-four — he was elected rabbi of one of the most influential Reform congregations, The Temple, in Cleveland, Ohio. His predecessor there, Moses Gries, was a Classical Reformer in every respect, including a marked coolness toward Zionism. That the congregation should select Silver, whose Zionism was certainly known to them, is the best indication of the reputation the young man had already gained as a most

14 Morgenstern to Silver, January 29, 1937, Papers, 29/674.
15 Michael A. Meyer, *Hebrew Union College-Jewish Institute of Religion: A Centennial History 1875–1975*, rev. ed., Cincinnati, 1992, pp. 131–132; Howard R. Greenstein, *Turning Point: Zionism and Reform Judaism*, Chico, CA, 1981, pp. 88–89.
16 A few months earlier Silver had suggested that Morgenstern (or Emil Leipziger or Jacob Marcus) might be appointed as one of the CCAR delegates to the American Jewish Conference in place of Rabbi Samuel Goldenson of Temple Emanu-El in New York, a leader of the American Council for Judaism. Silver to Solomon B. Freehof, July 29, 1943, Papers, 61/1446.
17 Silver to Joshua Liebman, November 3, 1943, Papers, 29/674.
18 He also implied that it would make contributions, not only to the College, but also to the Union of American Hebrew Congregations more difficult to obtain from Reform Zionists. Silver to Maurice N. Eisendrath, October 22, 1943, Papers, 61/1446.

capable religious leader and an extraordinarily talented orator. Still, the connection between Silver and The Temple was not easily made. While he was pressing his candidacy, questions were raised, presumably by leaders of the congregation, regarding his Zionism. In response, Silver wrote a most interesting letter to Gries. Since it represents the first extant elaboration of Silver's personal reconciliation of his Zionist and Reform views and helps us to understand his success in the Reform movement, it seems worthy of extended citation. The crucial sections of the letter read as follows:

> I believe that we are a people possessing spiritual uniqueness, dowered by Providence with a mission to serve mankind through religious leadership. This is primary and fundamental in my concept of Judaism. Else, I would not be in the ministry.
>
> The hope which prompts thousands of faithful Jews today to safe-guard their precious heritage, to intensify their Jewish life and to enrich its content by establishing a spiritual and cultural centre in Palestine cannot but meet with my sympathy and approval. Not that I see in the establishment of such a centre, a solution of all Jewish problems the world over, but that such a centre may be contributory towards a galvanization of Jewish life the world over — and any movement which aims at a deepening of Jewish consciousness and at a strengthening of Jewish spiritual solidarity cannot be foreign to me.
>
> For me the political phase of Zionism has at all times been secondary and incidental and with the emancipation of Russian Jewry, it has become negligible. I cannot grow enthusiastic over the establishment of a little Jewish state in Palestine. Should the nations of the world, however, at the conclusion of this war, favor the granting to the Jews in Palestine the privilege of political independence — and certain events seem to point in that direction — I cannot see where that would be detrimental either to their own welfare or to the status of the Jews in America or the world over.
>
> In this I am conscious of no double allegiance. I am in heart and soul an American; for I see in America the gradual unfolding of those divine principles of justice and righteousness for which my people has so bravely lived and suffered. The destiny of American Israel is, and must forever remain, interlaced with the destiny of America.
>
> And in conclusion, permit me to say, that in my humble opinion Zionism is *not* the vital problem of American Israel today. I hold that the significance of Zionism, as a political movement, has been over-estimated both by its friends and its enemies. The most pressing and perplexing problem which American Judaism faces is not Zionism — but religious apathy and indifference, frightful ignorance and lack of organization. Our problems are spiritual, pedagogic, administrative and we must solve them here and *now*.[19]

19 Silver to Moses J. Gries, April 26, 1917, Stephen S. Wise Papers, American Jewish Historical Society, Waltham, MA. I am grateful to Prof. Michael Brenner of Brandeis University for obtaining a copy of the letter.

Silver concluded that if his sentiments militated against "a mutual sympathy of pulpit and pew," he would prefer that his name be withdrawn from candidacy.

The letter apparently made Silver acceptable to both Gries and the board of The Temple. But when Stephen S. Wise visited Cleveland, he was shocked to learn how far the alleged Zionist, who as a boy in New York had founded the Dr. Herzl Zion Club, was willing to bend in order to gain the position. Initially, he had heartily congratulated the young rabbi and offered his assistance in all matters.[20] Now, to his dismay, he had learned that Silver's Zionism had "passed muster," that it was "so qualified as to be altogether unobjectionable." And he was not beyond a cynical insinuation: "I cannot believe that you have suffered such an impression to go out as would on any ground lead anyone to imagine that you would abate your devotion to Zionism in order to secure a pulpit on any extrinsic ground whatever."[21] In his response, Silver declared any imputation that he had modified his views to pass muster was "downright calumny and slander." There had been no conditions or tacit agreements. Yet, regrettably, the "nasty rumor" had spread widely. He assured Wise that he had been for years a disciple of Ahad Ha-Am and that he had come to Zionism "through my love of Hebrew Culture and Literature and for the mighty promises which it holds as a 'galvanizing force' in Jewish life."[22] He even sent Wise a copy of his letter to Gries. But it seems unlikely that Wise could have been persuaded by the Gries letter, which spoke of political Zionism as "secondary and incidental." As for Silver, he was deeply offended by Wise's almost unveiled suspicions. Later it was claimed by one of Wise's disciples that Silver never forgot the incident and never forgave Wise for it.[23]

Some time after Silver's "honeymoon" at The Temple, according to Vinograd, he received an order requiring him to cease giving Zionist sermons and engaging in nationalist activities. Thereupon, he relates, Silver immediately offered his resignation and forced the board to back down.[24] If the incident occurred as described,[25] it indicates not only that Silver, from the start, would not kowtow to the board, but also that in this very early test of wills he was able to make himself once-and-for-all master of the Temple,

20 Wise to Silver, April 28, 1917, Wise Papers.
21 Wise to Silver, May 7, 1917, in Carl Hermann Voss, ed., *Stephen S. Wise: Servant of the People, Selected Letters*, Philadelphia, 1969, pp. 78–80.
22 Silver to Wise, May 11, 1917, Wise Papers.
23 Morton Mayer Berman, *For Zion's Sake: A Personal and Family Chronicle*, Chicago, 1980, pp. 81–82.
24 Vinograd, *Abba Hillel Silver*, pp. 82–83.
25 Raphael, who examined the minutes of the congregation, makes no reference to it.

enjoying a position of unquestioned authority that he maintained easily thereafter throughout his rabbinical career. As would rapidly became apparent, Silver's Zionism was no barrier to his leadership either within his congregation or within the Reform movement.

Among his colleagues in the Reform rabbinate Silver was treated as a prodigy. Already in 1916, only a year after his ordination, he was called upon to address the annual convention of the Central Conference of American Rabbis (CCAR), the first of more than half a dozen sermons, lectures, and addresses that he would be asked to deliver to his assembled colleagues in succeeding years.[26] Unlike Wise, who rarely attended, Silver was usually present at CCAR conventions, even during those years when Zionist activity claimed most of his time.

To a Zionist colleague Silver confided that this attendance on the part of Zionist rabbis was essential to counterbalance the forces arrayed against them.[27] Yet already at this point in his career Silver was reluctant to introduce the divisive topic of Zionism into the deliberations of Reform rabbinical and lay bodies. He feared then, as he did later, that the chief result would be to give the anti-Zionists a platform for their views. They had more to gain by such debates than the Zionists, who could best manage their ascendancy without éclat.[28] In the 1920s he chose instead to work incrementally, inducing the CCAR to cooperate with the Palestine Development Council in the economic rehabilitation of Palestine and the promotion of Jewish settlement there.[29]

No less remarkable than Silver's early prominence among his rabbinical colleagues was his acclaim among the laity. As early as 1923, the now thirty-year-old rabbi was called upon to give the sermon at the Golden Jubilee Convention of the Union of American Hebrew Congregations meeting at Carnegie Hall in New York. During the 1920s and 30s he was inundated with speaking requests at a variety of Reform congregations. Perhaps most surprising are his repeated speaking appearances at Rockdale Avenue Temple in Cincinnati, whose rabbi was the very incarnation of American Reform anti-Zionism, David Philipson.[30]

---

26 Silver used the 1916 occasion, when he was asked to address "Religion and the Jewish Child," to argue that Jewish religious education should, in part, be concerned with making the child conscious of "an allegiance which he owes to a whole people." CCARY, vol. 26, 1916, p. 236.

27 Silver to Max Heller, March 26, 1919, Papers, 17/375.

28 Silver to Wise, May 18, 1920, Papers, 17/376.

29 Silver to Edward N. Calisch, October 18, 1921; Polish, *Renew Our Days*, pp. 157–161.

30 David Philipson to Silver, October 10, 1927, Papers, 193/98; Lester Jaffe to Silver, October 31, 1938, Papers, 193/99. The second occasion (and there may well have been others in-between) was to help celebrate Philipson's jubilee.

Silver's early broad acceptance within the Reform movement was due not only to his readiness to avoid harping on Zionism in his invited speeches; it was also attributable to a philosophy of Judaism which had as much or more in common with Reform anti-Zionists as it did with secular Jewish nationalists. Like Morgenstern,[31] Silver preached the advent of an "American Judaism" that would embrace the best elements of its German and East-European antecedents. From the former it would take prophetic idealism, from the latter warmth and mysticism. Like Isaac Mayer Wise, Silver was convinced (and it was not a view he ever gave up!) that, as he put it in 1919, "the golden period of Judaism in Spain will be as nothing compared to the golden period of Jewry in America in the days to come."[32] He was similarly persuaded of the glory of America which, created "by the grace of God," was destined to become "the great proving ground for the hopes of the world...the microcosm of which the whole of humanity is the macrocosm."[33] Such optimistic oratory was inspiring and inspiriting to his listeners, especially at a time, following World War I, when anti-Semitism and isolationism were running rampant. Speaking to the UAHC Jubilee convention in 1923 Silver said not a word about Zionism, certainly not that anti-Semitism should induce any reconsideration about Isaac Mayer Wise's ebullient hopes for America. His response to the recrudescence of hatred was pure Classical Reform in the tradition of David Einhorn: "We know that the world needs us most when it hates us most and so we shall continue to be the humble servants of the most High."[34]

Silver's Classical Reform Judaism found expression especially and persistently in his advocacy of the mission of Israel. This doctrine, not peculiar to Reform Judaism but fervently adopted by it, had long been a principal argument against Zionism. If Jews were to be a light unto the gentiles, how could they perform that task unless they were scattered among the nations. Zionism, it was argued, represented a withdrawal from the Jews' God-ordained mission. Silver was not the first Zionist in the Reform movement to reconcile the mission idea with Zionism by slightly modifying its doctrinal content. The Classical Reform rabbi of Chicago — and earliest of the Zionist rabbis in the movement — Bernhard Felsenthal had already

---

31 Meyer, *Hebrew Union College*, pp. 85–86.
32 Silver, "Isaac Mayer Wise: A Century of Reform Judaism," sermon delivered March 30, 1919, Papers, 145/45.
33 Silver, "What Has Become of the Melting Pot?" *The Temple*, vol. 4, no. 1 (n.d. but apparently 1922), p. 7.
34 Silver, "Our New Task," sermon delivered January 22, 1923, *The Temple*, vol. 4, no. 2, p. 8; the sermon was also printed in "Proceedings of the Twenty-Eighth Council of the Union of American Hebrew Congregations," *Proceedings of the Union of American Hebrew Congregations (PUAHC)*, pp. 9227–9231.

noted in 1897 that the mission of Israel among the nations could only be strengthened if there were a spiritual center in Palestine, and Stephen Wise had argued similarly that the diaspora mission of the Jew would continue in coordination with the Palestinian center.[35] Silver simply echoed that view more loudly. On the one hand, a nation did not need to be completely scattered to play the role of missionaries — it required a base and source of inspiration. But on the other, the Jewish people without the mission idea was doomed to insignificance. Silver put it most strongly in a sermon that he delivered at The Temple in 1926:

> It would be a mistake on the part of the champions of Jewish nationalism to push to the background this inspiring motif of Jewish life. I would not wish my people to become another statelet, another little Montenegro somewhere, merely for the sake of existing as a separate entity there. I wish my people to continue as a light-bringer unto mankind.[36]

Silver's defense of the mission concentrated more than that of his predecessors on the doctrine's roots in Prophetic and Pharisaic Judaism, its Jewish legitimacy. The idea became false only when it was deprived of the national foundation that was required to sustain it.[37] Most significantly, only the mission idea would preserve Judaism among Liberal Jews in the United States: "Even the strong appeal which Palestine is making today to many of our people will not prove sufficient to command their loyalty in the days to come."[38]

In these years Silver was not only an advocate of doctrinal Reform Judaism, he became its fervent defender against those who were subjecting it to attack. The major assault, in 1925 and 1926, came from a group of secularist Jews around the *Menorah Journal*: the talented Jewish intellectual Elliot E. Cohen, the advocate of a secular "Hebraism" Horace Kallen, and

---

35 On the earliest period see Michael A. Meyer, "American Reform Judaism and Zionism: Early Efforts at Ideological Rapprochement," *Studies in Zionism*, No. 7, Spring 1983, pp. 49–64.

36 Weiner, ed., *Therefore Choose Life*, p. 216.

37 Silver, "The Democratic Impulse in Jewish History," CCARY, vol. 38, 1928, pp. 199–216. This lecture was even reprinted almost in full and with approbation in the February 1930 issue of *The Liberal Jewish Monthly*, the distinctly anti-Zionist organ of British Liberal Judaism. In introducing the piece, its editor noted that "When the Zionist insists that a Jew must be a Jew by religion, then he is at one with Liberal Judaism in the most fundamental issue."

38 Silver, "Why Do the Heathen Rage," originally printed in installments in *Jewish Tribune*, July 23, July 30, August 6, and August 13, 1926, and then as a pamphlet, where the citation occurs on p. 22.

the editor of the journal Henry Hurwitz. These men mercilessly indicted religious Judaism, the synagogue, and the rabbinate. They particularly reveled in subjecting the cherished mission of Israel to merciless ridicule. Few Reform rabbis were as equipped as Silver to rise to the defense. He possessed *bona fides* both as a scholar and a Zionist and he could hold his own in any debate. In response to the raging of the "heathen," as Silver dubbed this group, he drew back from Ahad Ha-Am and argued that Judaism had survived on account of its religion, not its culture, and only the Jewish religion would preserve it in the future. And that religion would be passionately held by Jews only if they believed in the mission of Israel.[39]

Silver's strong conviction — frequently expressed in the interwar years — that the only true Judaism was religious Judaism was reflected in the decision of his congregation in 1929 to eliminate all secular activities in the temple building, a decision that could hardly have been made without his approval. The purpose of a synagogue, he believed, was to concentrate on religious worship and education.[40] Not surprisingly, Silver also defended the mission idea when Mordecai Kaplan declared it both dangerous and absurd.[41] It was no more absurd than the words of the Prophets, Silver declared, and if it was dangerous as an advocate for Judaism to take on Trinitarian Christianity as well as all forms of social privilege, then, Silver insisted, one should be prepared to live dangerously.[42]

It would be a mistake to conclude, however, that Silver's Zionism in the 1920s had fallen silent. From time to time he spoke on the subject from the pulpit or wrote on it in an article. He stressed the centrality of Palestine in Jewish history and in contemporary Jewish life. Yet what is clear from these expressions is that Silver continued to be, as he had said in the letter to Wise of 1917, a cultural rather than a political Zionist. Although he recognized the need for a refuge for persecuted Jews, Silver would not raise that goal to the status of ideology:

A people that constructs a life philosophy on suffering is a neurotic people, and I would be humiliated if the only claim which Israel had upon me was the fact of its age-old suffering and martyrdom. It isn't the misery of our people which makes Palestine a burning issue today, nor is it anti-Semitism.... It is not the persecuted bodies of my people that need Palestine so much as the

39 Ibid., p. 24.
40 Herbert Weiner, ed., *A Word in its Season: Selected Sermons, Addresses, and Writings of Abba Hillel Silver*, vol. 2, New York and Cleveland, 1972, p. 316.
41 Cf. Mordecai M. Kaplan, *Judaism as a Civilization: Toward a Reconstruction of American-Jewish Life* (1934), New York, 1967, p. 113; but Silver cites from an earlier writing.
42 Silver, "The Democratic Impulse," pp. 215–216.

persecuted and harassed spirit of the race that needs a refuge and a sanctuary....
At no time was the spirit of our race so much in danger by compromising and
fawning and cringing as at the present time, and we want a home for this soul
of our race where it can live in a congenial environment, where it can create
and evolve new and finer spiritual and cultural values with which to bless
mankind in the future even as it has blessed mankind in the past.[43]

Silver would return to the Herzlian Zionism of his early youth only when
Nazism made that imperative.

The Zionism Battle in the CCAR

When the Committee on Synagogue Music made its report at the
convention of the Central Conference of American Rabbis in 1930, it was
not expected to cause controversy. But, extraordinarily, Stephen S. Wise was
present for the convention and chose to make an issue of what he regarded as
a serious omission: the words and music of "Hatikvah" would not appear in
the revised hymnal. When it became known to him that "The Star Spangled
Banner" would appear, Wise went into a diatribe and forced a recorded vote
of the plenum, which — remarkably — resulted in 65 votes in favor and 59
against.[44] The Jewish press responded favorably to this expression of Zionist
sympathy, seeing it as a symbol of increasing Jewish unity on the Zionist
issue.[45]

Silver was not present at the 1930 convention. However, a few months
later, he received an extraordinary letter circulated to the entire CCAR by
the chairman of the committee revising the hymnal, Rabbi Louis Wolsey. A
confirmed anti-Zionist, Wolsey used the occasion to vent his spleen on the
Zionism that was infiltrating the CCAR[46] by subjecting "Hatikvah" to
vigorous denigration: it was musically unworthy; "inspired by some Slavic or
Spanish drinking song,...an undevotional and non-religious poem;...
completely counter to the theology of the Union Prayer Book;...its inclusion
definitely commits the American Jew to the singing of two national
anthems;...[and] many laymen of the Reform synagogue have already stated
that they would not permit the new Union Hymnal to be used in their

43 Silver, "My Dream of Palestine," *Jewish Tribune*, June 13, 1924, vol. 2. Cf. Daniel Jeremy
   Silver, ed., *In the Time of Harvest: Essays in Honor of Abba Hillel Silver on the Occasion of His
   70th Birthday*, New York and London, 1963, pp. 33–36.
44 CCARY, vol. 40, 1930, pp. 89–108.
45 Solomon Freehof to Abba Hillel Silver, October 27, 1930, Papers, 18/387.
46 "Wolsey has a very definite persecution mania in regard to Zionism." James Heller to Silver,
   October 30, 1930, Papers, 18/387.

congregations if Hatikwah [sic] is to be included." For these reasons all members of the CCAR were asked to send in their straw votes on the subject to the chairman. Wolsey did note that such a mail vote could not overturn the decision of the convention, but his intent was clearly to undermine its representativeness so that it could be overturned the following year. Ten members of the committee signed Wolsey's letter; Rabbis Jacob Singer, Morris Lazaron (then still in his Zionist period), James G. Heller, and Solomon Freehof did not.[47]

When Silver received the letter, he sent off a telegram to the president of the CCAR, Rabbi David Lefkowitz, registering his "vigorous protest" that such a letter could have been sent, declaring it "unwarranted, illegal and a clear challenge to the sovereignty of the convention," and asking him to repudiate it immediately.[48] Yet it is interesting that when Lazaron suggested to Silver that the "Hatikvah" controversy should lead to a more general confrontation in which Zionists and anti-Zionists in the CCAR would finally have it out at the next convention, Silver balked. "It seems that a battle is inevitable," he replied to Lazaron, "and if it must come the Hatikwah [sic] might as well serve for a battle-field as anything else." But then he added that good tactics would require allowing the anti-Zionists to take the offensive. He was convinced that majority control had already passed to the Zionists: "Let the anti-Zionists bring the matter up again, if they want, at the next convention of the Conference. They will be licked again."[49]

Not only were they licked again, they were trounced. In what was likely a stratagem to gain victory on a revote, Wolsey ruled that the Conference's will, expressed at the last convention, required that all verses of "Hatikvah" be included in the hymnal. But when this bloated proposal was brought to a vote, it was adopted by a voice vote and the succeeding motion to exclude the five-versed "Hatikvah" lost on a roll call vote 41 to 54. Silver had opposed taking the second vote, desiring both to let the decision of the previous year stand and to avoid division.[50]

---

47 Louis Wolsey to Members of the Central Conference of American Rabbis, September 30, 1930, Papers, 18/387.
48 Silver to David Lefkowitz, October 24, 1930, Papers, 18/387. When Wolsey threatened to resign as chairman of the committee, Lefkowitz dissociated himself from Silver's language, declaring the circular letter simply "unwise" and Wolsey decided to stay on. Silver upbraided Lekfkowitz for backing down and sought to exercise pressure by threatening to bring the matter up at the next convention unless the Executive Board of the Conference took action against the chairman. But this was not a serious threat. As indicated below, Silver did not want to divide the Conference. Silver to Lefkowitz, November 28, 1930, Lefkowitz to Silver, December 2, 1930, Papers, 18/387.
49 Silver to Morris S. Lazaron, October 31, 1930, Papers 18/387.
50 CCARY, vol. 41, 1931, pp. 98, 102–104, 114–117.

But divisions within the CCAR were becoming ever more profound as the Zionist rabbis emerged more clearly as the majority and the remaining anti-Zionists and non-Zionists felt increasingly pressed to the wall. Following the votes on "Hatikvah," the next Zionist-related issue to come before the Conference was one that brought the rabbis into internal Zionist politics. In 1934 Rabbi Samuel Wohl of Cincinnati, the president of the League for Labor Palestine, asked Rabbi Edward Israel to draw up a statement favoring the Labor movement in Palestine that would obtain as many CCAR signatures as possible. Publication of the statement would be timed to coincide with Jabotinsky's visit to the United States and would, by implication, imply a rejection of Revisionism even as it was, in content, an identification with the principles of the Histadrut. Silver signed on as a member of the endorsing committee, along with fellow Zionists in the Reform rabbinate and Hebrew Union College faculty members Jacob Marcus and Nelson Glueck. The statement, which identified the program of the Histadrut with the principles of Prophetic Judaism, secured 241 signatures, at that time over 60 per cent of the Conference, including men who were not avid Zionists. When the statement was published a few weeks later together with a similar one by Conservative rabbis, Stephen S. Wise wrote a foreword in which he declared the two statements "destined to become historic."[51] Nonetheless, shortly after the statement was circulated, it was viciously attacked by a disciple and close associate of Wise, Rabbi Louis I. Newman, the most prominent Revisionist in the CCAR. Newman had sought in vain to prevent issuance of the statement and then, with almost no success, appealed to rabbis who had signed it to repudiate their signatures. Rabbi Israel, who was active both as an advocate of social justice and as a Zionist, responded that the ideas it expressed seemed appropriate for the CCAR, which had long criticized economic inequality in the United States. Silver, a General Zionist, supported the statement rather than place himself in opposition to a declaration that linked Reform Jewish values, to which he subscribed, with those of the socialist Histadrut.[52]

The famed debate on Zionism at the convention of the CCAR the following year has been seen as "truly a meeting of giants," with the old forces of anti-Zionism, represented by its most articulate spokesman, Rabbi Samuel Schulman of Temple Emanu-El in New York, arrayed against the strongly emergent Zionism within the Reform rabbinate championed by

---

51 *The Rabbis of America to Labor Palestine*, New York, 1935, p. 5. See also Wise's editorial on the Jabotinsky visit in *Opinion*, January 1935, pp. 5–6.
52 Edward L. Israel to Silver, October 18, 1934; Israel and endorsing committee to colleagues, December 8, 1934; Israel to Silver, February 8, 1935, Papers, 18/391.

Abba Hillel Silver.[53] Silver himself claimed correctly that "it was at this Conference that the opposition of the Central Conference of American Rabbis to Zionism was finally officially abandoned" and "replaced by a position of benevolent neutrality."[54]

Yet the "debate" itself, which was followed by a discussion that went on long into the night, was full of paradoxes and ironies. It was the third of three discussions scheduled respectively on the subjects of God, Torah, and Israel, with an eye to formulating a revised platform for the Reform movement.[55] Born in 1864 and Silver's elder by almost thirty years, Samuel Schulman was indeed a representative of the "older generation." He was certainly a Classical Reformer, but he was hardly a fervent anti-Zionist. As early as 1918 he had written to Lina Straus, a prominent Zionist member of his congregation who accused him of undermining Zionist efforts, that although he refused "to recognize Palestine as a homeland for *the* Jewish people, for the whole Jewish nation," he did recognize "the tremendous importance of what the Allies are doing with respect to the promise of Palestine to the Jews." He was not a Zionist because he was opposed to a secular Jewish nationalism that would render Israel no different from other nations and because he chose to emphasize Jewish religion rather than nationality.[56] By 1935 he had come considerably closer to Zionism. To be sure, he still spoke of the Jewish entity as Keneset Yisrael and firmly rejected Mordecai Kaplan's idea that Judaism was a civilization in which religion was optional for contemporary participants in it. But, in contrast to Silver, he stressed the importance of a return to Jewish "individuality," by which he meant the particularism of Judaism expressed through "the fruitful power of the ceremonial law as a discipline and a hallowing and purifying influence in our lives."[57] In the debate it was Schulman, not Silver, who made settlement in Palestine a trying but necessary challenge specifically for Reform Jews. "Palestine will lead to a new synthesis," he expounded, and therefore "Reform Judaism has the grandest opportunity in its history; it has the opportunity of martyrdom [!]. Let it send half a dozen young men or more to Palestine to bring the message of Progressive Judaism." And he called for a religiously based Zionist commitment: "Let us also feel that Palestine is a

---

53 Joseph L. Blau in the volume he edited, *Reform Judaism: A Historical Perspective. Essays from the Yearbook of the Central Conference of American Rabbis*, New York, 1973, pp. 369–370. See also the more nuanced interpretation by Alexander Schindler in Raphael, *Abba Hillel Silver*, pp. xxvi–xxviii.

54 Autobiography/memoirs, Papers 211/1, p. 9K.

55 Felix Levy to Silver, November 1, 1934, Papers 18/391.

56 Samuel Schulman to Lina Straus, September 10, 1918, Schulman Papers, American Jewish Archives (hereafter AJA). I am grateful to Mark Strauss-Cohn for this reference.

57 In Blau, ed., *Reform Judaism*, p. 412.

field for us.... Not to stand aloof is our aim, but recognizing the value of Palestine for hundreds of thousands of our brethren in Israel, let us help increase the settlement and, at the same time, let us bravely uphold the truth that Israel is not a Goy like other Goyim."[58]

Silver's lengthy, carefully balanced oration offered no such inspiration. It was more a historical overview of the subject than a call to Zionist colors. Like Schulman, he argued for the centrality and indispensability of religion in Judaism and its necessity for Jewish survival, at least in the Diaspora.[59] He did not make a case specifically for political, or even for cultural Zionism. His opposition was directed against those who attempted "to substitute a part for the whole." They might be the pure religionists (whom he compared with Paul) or the secular nationalists; both presented only a partial view of "the total program of Jewish life," which embraced the religious mandate of mission as well as the national aspirations of the Jewish people.[60]

During the next two years Silver served as a member of the committee that drew up the Columbus Platform, adopted by the CCAR in 1937. As is well known, that platform used the language of Herzl and Ahad Ha-Am in advocating the creation of a Palestine that was a "Jewish homeland" and haven of refuge and also a "center of Jewish culture and spiritual life." As a member of the committee, Silver may have played a role in preventing any less Zionistic language. When its chairman, the Hebrew Union College theologian and cultural Zionist Samuel S. Cohon, suggested that much acrimony could be avoided by omitting the phrase "a Jewish homeland," Silver apparently refused to accede and Cohon accepted the position of the "orthodox Zionists" in the CCAR.[61] Indeed, by 1937 even David Philipson, also a member of the committee, was willing, at least reluctantly, to accept the idea of a homeland in Palestine. Zionist conceptions were making rapid progress among the Reform rabbis, in part — but only in part — due to Silver's efforts. The support of the younger rabbinical generation was there in any case. It was only in the area of Zionist political policy where serious differences among Reform religious and lay leaders remained and where they would soon rise to the surface, resulting in a degree of acrimony that was unprecedented in earlier debates. During these years — the early 1940s — Silver became vice-president and then president of the CCAR at the same

---

58   Ibid., pp. 413–414.
59   In a sermon three years earlier he had declared that cultural pluralism in America was "a vain and hopeless dream." Cultural Jews would inevitably assimilate; only religious Jews would remain. Weiner, ed., *Therefore Choose Life*, p. 391.
60   In Blau, ed., *Reform Judaism*, pp. 435–436.
61   Samuel S. Cohon to Silver, May 14, 1937, Cohon Papers, AJA, MSS Col. 276, 2/6. Silver apparently ignores Cohon's plea in his reply to him four days later although he comments on other portions of the platform draft that Cohon had enclosed.

time that he was the most prominent and effective champion of an uncompromising insistence on Jewish statehood.

ACJ and AJC

Beginning in the late 1930s, paradoxically, Silver's criticism of nationalist excess became more vocal in response to Nazism even as his Zionism came to focus on a political goal. Speaking to the graduating class at Hebrew Union College in 1936, Silver branded fascism the "new paganism" and deplored the nationalism "which has more or less run riot in the modern world." Yet at the same time, with the increasingly precarious situation of the Jews in Germany and, later, the rest of the European continent, he was forced to turn more vigorously to the political Zionism of his youth, distinguishing it from other forms of national aspiration that clearly contravened Jewish religion and morality. He told the ordinees:

> The rabbi should encourage the co-operation of his people in up-building the Jewish Homeland in Palestine..., because a Jewish homeland will help to normalize the status of our people in the world, because it will remove the element of desperation — of fighting with our backs to the wall — from our renewed struggle for equality and emancipation..., because it will serve as haven for hosts of our people who must now seek new homes in a world where doors are everywhere closing.

Only as a last reason for supporting Zionism did Silver list his hope that "this Jewish Homeland may become in the days to come a vast dynamo of creative Jewish cultural and spiritual energies."[62] But even more now, at least to Reform audiences, Silver criticized Jewish spokesmen who offered a Jewish nationalism that substituted for Judaism a nationalism that was "unredeemed by a moral vision and responsibility" or which neglected the spiritual needs of Jews in the diaspora. Jewish nationalism, in Silver's view, had to be distinctly different from the fascist variety; it had to be guided by the prophetic ethics long stressed by Reform Judaism.[63]

It was this unwavering loyalty to Reform ideology that continued to make Silver *persona grata* within Reform rabbinical and lay circles even as he became ever more visible within world Zionism. In 1943, when he was head of the American Zionist Emergency Council, Silver was elected unanimously

---

62 "The Ancient Paths," in Weiner, ed., *Therefore Choose Life*, pp. 423, 426.
63 "Religion in Present-Day Jewish Life," *PUAHC*, Thirty-Sixth Biennial Council, Cincinnati, 1939, p. 249.

to the vice presidency of the CCAR and thereby virtually assured of the presidency two years later.[64] During the years of his CCAR presidency, 1945–1947, he also served as president of the Zionist Organization of America. In order to carry out his Zionist and congregational duties along with the CCAR presidency, Silver delegated day-to-day tasks of the office to his vice president, boyhood friend and fervent admirer, Rabbi Abraham Feldman — which seems not to have stirred up resentment, although Feldman's candidacy for the vice-presidency had provoked unusual controversy.[65]

It was in 1942, the year before Silver's election to the CCAR vice-presidency, that the last great Zionist controversy within the Reform rabbinate occurred. At issue was a proposal for the CCAR to support the demand that the Jewish population of Palestine be given the privilege of establishing a military force that would fight under its own banner on the side of the Allies. The existence of such a force, all realized, would be a strong argument for Jewish sovereignty following the war. When the resolution passed by a vote of 64 to 38, the American Reform rabbinate had placed itself on the side of maximal Zionist ambitions. It had also seriously alienated about a fifth of the Conference, men who now went on to form the American Council for Judaism (ACJ), dedicated to combating "the political emphasis now paramount in the Zionistic program."

Silver's attitude to his colleagues who joined the ACJ was uncompromising. Although he did not attack them personally, as did Stephen S. Wise, he refused to sit down with them at a meeting intended to bring reconciliation[66] and did not support Solomon Freehof's attempts at mediation. To Freehof he wrote in regard to Wise's attack on ACJ members Fineshriber and Wolsey: "Rabbis who enter the political arena must be prepared to receive blows even as they give them, and should not turn squeamish when the blows which they receive are resounding ones."[67] Later, as president of the CCAR, Silver suggested that the 1943 resolution of the CCAR, which urged members to seek termination of the ACJ, should now,

64 Transcript: "Transactions of the CCAR, 54th Annual Convention, New York City, June 22–27, 1943," AJA, MSS Col. 34, Box 37, p. 296.

65 In 1945 there were no counter-nominations to Silver for president either by mail or from the floor. But two non-Zionist rabbis, Louis Mann and Jonah B. Wise, were nominated by mail and Jacob Marcus from the floor for the vice-presidency. In a secret ballot Feldman won handily, receiving more votes than the combined total of his opponents. Transcript: "Proceedings of the 56th Annual Convention of the CCAR," Atlantic City, June 25–27, 1945, AJA, MSS Col. 34, Box 37, pp. 231, 257–268. Cf. CCARY, vol. 55, 1945, pp. 172–174, where the controversy is only hinted at.

66 Greenstein, Turning Point, pp. 95, 156.

67 Wise to Freehof, November 24, 1944, Papers 29/674.

given its unfortunate and politically pernicious continuance, be understood to imply immediate dissociation from it.[68]

Silver was similarly resolute but more compromising with regard to residual opposition to political Zionism's contemporary aims among the Reform laity. The Union of American Hebrew Congregations had participated in the American Jewish Conference of 1943 and, unlike the American Jewish Committee, not bolted when that conference, influenced decisively by Silver's oratory, passed a resolution calling for the establishment of a Jewish commonwealth. But it did abstain on the crucial vote, claiming the need to seek approval from the UAHC Executive Board. Following the sessions of the conference, prominent laymen within the movement, marshaled by Judge Horace Stern of Philadelphia, put pressure on Rabbi Maurice Eisendrath, the UAHC's newly elected vigorous executive director, to categorically dissent from the Palestine resolution of the Conference, especially as abstention was being widely interpreted as concurrence. Zionists, including Silver, wanted the Executive Board to ratify it. Fearing public controversy, which could only weaken his efforts to expand the Union, Eisendrath turned to Silver just before the scheduled meeting of the board urging his endorsement of a compromise board resolution that he had worked out together with Solomon Freehof. Endorsement of a Jewish commonwealth, Eisendrath argued, would never pass the board as presently constituted. Moreover, silence would strengthen the ACJ. He promised, for the future, to work at shuffling the composition of the Union's board to make it more reflective of pro-Zionist sentiment among Reform congregants. Silver, however, was deaf to Eisendrath's plea. In a strongly worded reply he argued that a resolution of non-concurrence would be interpreted as repudiation so that Reform Judaism would "again remain an isolated sect within the stream of American Jewish life."[69] He threatened to resign from the Executive Board, of which he was an ex-officio member by virtue of his vice-presidency of the CCAR. But Silver, too, realized that the votes for an endorsement were not there and he too did not want to provoke public controversy. His own compromise was that the Executive Board would defer decision to the next biennial meeting of the full Council. Silence, at least for the present, was preferable to taking a chance on defeat. When the Executive Board met a few days later and found itself divided almost equally

---

68 CCARY, vol. 56, 1946, pp. 226–227.
69 Silver to Eisendrath, September 29, 1943, Papers 61/1446. When Stern turned to Silver, he replied similarly and added: "It is a fatal blunder to shackle Reform Judaism forever with a complex of ideas, which were always foreign to historic Judaism and to the historic aspirations of the Jewish people, and which having had their brief day among sections of Jews in Western Europe, finally suffered defeat with the destruction of that Jewry itself." Silver to The Honorable Judge Horace Stern, October 1, 1943, Papers 61/1446.

between ratification and repudiation, it voted, as Silver had earlier suggested and as he urged at the meeting, in favor of postponement until the next meeting of the Council.[70]

That should have put the matter to rest for a while. However, when pressure continued and Eisendrath began to fear a schism within the Union, he decided to call an informal meeting of rabbis to recommend a program of action to the smaller Administrative Committee of the Union, which was to meet on November 30. Some statement of neutrality, Eisendrath thought, was necessary if the Union were both to remain within the American Jewish Conference and hold itself together. Silver was not persuaded, and he did not attend the meeting. Eighteen out of the twenty-six invitees, however, did. Freehof presided over a group with widely differing views on Zionism[71] that adopted a resolution which left controversial Zionist issues up to the individual Reform Jew and declared that the Union, although remaining in the Conference, was unable to associate itself with those parts of the Palestine Resolution that called for exclusive Jewish control of immigration into Palestine and the establishment of a Jewish Commonwealth. With the endorsement of the Administrative Committee, this resolution went to the Executive Board. Here Silver was present. Considering that he had wanted the UAHC to endorse the Palestine resolution, his principal statement to the group was a bit disingenuous, but factually it was truthful:

> I have never, in all my ministry, come to a Union meeting and urged that we adopt a Zionist platform. I have never come to the CCAR and urged them to adopt a Zionist platform. I never urged my own congregation to adopt a Zionist platform.... The attempt that has been made in the last year and a half, with all the best intentions in the world, to bring Zionists and non-Zionists together on a common platform was doomed to failure, because it is clear that Zionists and non-Zionists, if they are to agree at all, must agree on a non-Zionist platform, and the Zionists will never agree to a non-Zionist platform.[72]

---

70 Proceedings of the Executive Board, October 3, 1943, *PUAHC*, Cincinnati, 1943, pp. 110–111.

71 Among the Zionists present was Felix Levy who, like Eisendrath, was determined to preserve the UAHC from division by avoiding pro-Zionist or anti-Zionist endorsements. Silver, however, was shocked that Levy could support the sense of the meeting. He wrote to him afterwards that he was sure a resolution dissociating the Union from the Palestine resolution would be interpreted as nothing less than repudiation of free immigration and political sovereignty, which he now declared "two basic Zionist principles." Levy to Eisendrath, December 3, 1943; Silver to Levy, December 17, 1943, Papers, 61/1146.

72 Proceedings of the Executive Board, January 18, 1944, *PUAHC*, Cincinnati, 1947, p. 29. Cf. Samuel Halperin, *The Political World of American Zionism*, Detroit, 1961, pp. 243–244, and Greenstein, *Turning Point*, pp. 96–97, 107–108, which, however, are not accurate on all points.

Following a brief discussion, Silver was selected to participate in a broadly representative drafting committee, which came up with a new resolution. This one, unlike that passed by the Administrative Committee, did not make reference to immigration and sovereignty and it did not use the language "unable to associate itself with," substituting instead "refrains from taking any action on the Palestine Resolution." The new resolution passed 22 to 2, only Julian Morgenstern and the vigorously anti-Zionist layman Gustave Efroymson voting in the negative. For Silver it was a minor victory. The new wording was less subject to misinterpretation. Even if the Union was not ready to adopt the two controversial points of the Palestine resolution, neither was its stand embarrassing to Silver in his position of Zionist leadership. Although Reform Judaism and Zionism were fused in Silver's own ideology, organizationally it was still best to keep them apart.

Reform Judaism and the State of Israel

With the establishment of the Jewish state, Silver might have been expected to settle there. For a variety of political and personal reasons he did not. But even as he remained in Cleveland, he repeatedly explained the significance of Israel for diaspora Jews. His answer was always more or less the same: the establishment of the Jewish state meant an end to *galut* even for the Jews outside its borders and therefore it was an "epochal event" for all Jews. Henceforth they would everywhere possess self-respect, security, and normality.

After 1948 Silver returned once more from Herzl to Ahad Ha-Am, even admitting that "the East rather than the West will again become the decisive cultural milieu of the creative Jewish life of tomorrow."[73] Israel would be, as it was in ancient times, "the non-political center of world Jewry." But even the establishment of the state did not invalidate the mission of Israel in the diaspora. On the contrary, its existence made possible the redirection of diaspora Jewish energies from life saving and state building to synagogues, schools and academies in the diaspora. And, although Israel might now be the focus of world Jewry, America could become "a great creative center of Jewish spiritual life" and the Jews there "a light unto the nations." Employing a term that would become common usage to describe the relationship between Israel and American Jewry, he spoke of their "interdependence."

As long as he was in a position of Zionist leadership, Silver had said little about the religious future of the state of Israel, perhaps because he did not

---

73 "Liberal Judaism and Israel" (Address Delivered at the Fortieth Biennial Assembly of the Union of American Hebrew Congregations in Boston, November 1948), in Abba Hillel Silver, *Vision and Victory: A Collection of Addresses*, New York, 1949, p. 222.

want to lose the support of the Mizrachi party.[74] But after 1948 he spoke freely of the need for "a vital Liberal Judaism" in the new state in order to sustain its spiritual morale. He looked for a native Israeli expression of Reform Judaism, declaring: "We cannot import our special brand of reform Judaism into Israel. Our spiritual apparel may not be suitable raiment for them."[75] Nonetheless, in essence it would closely resemble his own Classical Reform outlook in that its chief characteristics would be prophetic idealism rather than attention to ritual and tradition.[76]

Although he did not settle in Israel himself, Silver hoped that younger Jewish diaspora idealists would make aliyah. He visited often himself, now unabashedly as a rabbi. At the dedication of Kfar Silver in 1956 he called himself *rav umoreh beyisrael* (rabbi and teacher in Israel) and offered a prayer to God for the agricultural school's welfare.[77] Theologically, Silver remained uncertain as to whether the restoration of the state possessed religious significance. In the early 1950s he thought that it had not altered the religious destiny of the Jewish people. It was national restoration, not religious redemption; freedom from *shibud malkhuyot* (political subjection), not *aharit ha-yamim* (the End of Days). As the culmination of the particularist thrust in Judaism, it made possible a renewed turning toward the universal messianic goal.[78] But by the time Israel was a decade old, Silver was ready to tell his rabbinical colleagues that the establishment of the state was an act in the continuing drama of universal salvation, a link between God's covenant with Abraham and the final messianic *ge'ulah shelemah* (complete redemption).[79]

Still, the 1950s in Silver's life most closely resembled the 1920s. Once again he focused on America with the same optimism about its future and the future of its Jewish community that he had expressed thirty years earlier. He had not lost Isaac Mayer Wise's ebullient hopes for American Judaism. Israel might be the principal spiritual center, but he did not see American Jewry as on the periphery.[80] Within Reform circles he was now, more than ever, a source of pride. He was the only strongly identified Reform rabbi who had played a major role in Jewish political history.

74 Polish, *Renew Our Days*, p. 122.
75 "The Problems Which Lie Ahead," CCARY, vol. 68, 1958, p. 302.
76 Silver, *Vision and Victory*, p. 230.
77 Vinograd, *Abba Hillel Silver*, pp. 450–452.
78 Silver, "Problems and Prospects of American Judaism" (Founder's Day Address at the Hebrew Union College, March 12, 1950); Silver, "There is Yet Room for Vision" (Commencement Address at the Hebrew Union College-Jewish Institute for Religion, June 7, 1952) in Weiner, ed., *Therefore Choose Life*, pp. 411, 434–435.
79 "The Problems Which Lie Ahead," CCARY, vol. 68, 1958, p. 295.
80 CCARY, 60, 1950, p. 368; "On the Threshold of the Fourth Century" (Address Delivered at the Biennial Convention of the Union of American Hebrew Congregations in New York, April 1953), in *The Temple Bulletin*, Cleveland, May 17, 1953, pp. 5–8.

In Sum

Abba Hillel Silver did not conquer Reform Judaism for Zionism. Its gradual adoption of Zionist principles was underway before his time and was influenced by other factors, including the influx of East European Jews into the rabbinate and laity of the movement, the maturing of the settlement in Palestine, and the rise of Nazism. But surely Silver, a Jew deeply and fully committed to the principles of Reform Judaism, played a role in that development by demonstrating through his writings, speeches, and activities that Reform Judaism was compatible with Zionism.

It is somewhat ironic that this role should have been played by a Reform Jew who remained attached to the Classical Reform tradition and spurned its revision in other areas than Zionism. Silver was not enamored of Reform Judaism's return to ritualism;[81] he thought that the postwar emphasis on social justice was exaggerated; he did not adopt the increasing role of the rabbi as pastor; and — always the individualist — he rejected progressive egalitarianism in the administration of the CCAR.[82] In his ever rebounding optimism about American Jewry he resembled no one more than Isaac Mayer Wise. His theism, firmly rooted in the Prophets and the Pharisees, ran counter to more recent trends in the movement that looked to humanist thinkers or religious existentialists.[83] His emphasis on understanding Judaism historically, which he believed was the most secure foundation for Zionism, had its origins in the Wissenschaft des Judentums that he first encountered as a student at Hebrew Union College.

Yet Silver well recognized that Reform was only one interpretation of Judaism, that it served only one group of Jews. Zionism enabled him to transcend its confines even as he remained within its organizational framework. Although he did not force Zionist commitments upon fellow Reformers, he preached Zionism in their midst; although he did not appear as a Reform rabbi in Zionist parleys, he lent religious fervor to the movement. These two spheres of his activity were not compartmentalized in his Jewish worldview. In philosophy, if not in program, he was a religious Zionist not less than any member of Mizrachi, except that in his case the religion was Reform Judaism.

---

81 In his congregation he did reintroduce the Friday evening and Saturday morning services and the teaching of Hebrew, but he kept the Sunday morning service as the principal religious activity of the week and saw little value in the reintroduction of "discarded rituals."

82 See Silver's notes for the 1963 dialogue with Freehof in Papers, 187/1044.

83 CCARY, vol. 57, 1947, p. 391; Feuer, "The Influence of Abba Hillel Silver," p. 96.

Silver and Ben-Gurion: Two Types of Leadership

Anita Shapira

THE HISTORICAL MEMORY OF NATIONS AND PEOPLES tends to be short. Ben-Gurion, however, has been accorded a well-preserved niche in Israeli collective memory, being inseparable from the foundation myth of the state. Nevertheless, it is doubtful that the name of one of the greatest of leaders to emerge in American Jewry, Abba Hillel Silver, is sustained in the collective memory of modern American Jews. Does this reflect a certain paucity of historical consciousness among American Jews? In this paper, I will contend that the oblivion into which Silver has fallen is the result of his particular mode of leadership, compared with that of Ben-Gurion.

We do not have to be students of semiotics to appreciate the importance of photographic images as a valuable historical source. Photos of Ben-Gurion and Silver give us a wealth of pictorial information on the two men. Ben-Gurion was of short stature and ungainly, his body movements sharp and rapid, his dress informal, plebeian: in the 1920s while he served as the secretary general of the Histadrut, it was his wont to wear a Russian rubashka, fastened with a cord around his waist — the tunic of the revolutionaries. Later, as the chair of the Zionist Executive and engaged in negotiations with the British authorities, he conceded to putting on a suit, although he usually avoided a necktie and wore his collar open. In his final years in Sde Boker, as a kind of protest against bourgeois propriety, he used to wear khaki. Perhaps this was a way to express his sense of kibbutz simplicity; maybe it was an allusion to a military uniform. In any case, Ben-Gurion was never concerned about his external image, and there was always a spark of the young revolutionary about him, some element that despised the conventions of bourgeois society.

By contrast, Silver was extremely meticulous about his dress and personal appearance: tall and physically attractive, he had a dignified bearing and was a practiced master of the art of body language. From his youth, he adopted the elegant dress characteristic of Christian clergymen: a black, well-tailored suit, white shirt and carefully chosen tie — the standard apparel of the American middle class. His photos radiate gravity and respectability, strength of character and self-confidence. It would be hard to find two other public figures so diametrically different from one another in physical appearance. The message conveyed by their appearance should not be lost on us.

It has been said that history boiled down is nothing but biography. Perhaps comparative biography can provide us with additional insight. An examination of the biographical data of the early years of these two leaders turns up a strong similarity. Ben-Gurion was born in 1886 in Plonsk, 60 kilometers from Warsaw, Silver in 1893 in Lithuania, not far from the Prussian border. Both were born in the Pale of Settlement, into the well-knit and consolidated fabric of Jewish life, a society rooted in Orthodox religious observance and traditional Jewish learning. It is true that new winds of change had begun to blow. But those currents were more evident in the larger cities and did not confound the tranquility of life in the small towns and villages. The family environments of the two boys were not marked by Orthodox zeal. Rather, a spirit of *maskiliut balebatit* (petit bourgois enlightenment) pervaded their homes, and an evident leaning toward Zionism.

Only seven years separated them, and their social backgrounds were clearly similar. Ben-Gurion's father was what was called a *Winkeladvokat* — a kind of public notary whose function was to record petitions and agreements at the courthouse. The Green family belonged to the lower middle class. The Silver family was also part of the declining middle-class. Silver's father was involved in the manufacture of soaps and cosmetics. The process of rapid industrialization that swept across areas of the Pale had undermined the position of traditional artisans engaged in small-scale production, and the Silver family was plunged into poverty. This economic factor was central in motivating Silver's father to emigrate to the United States. In New York, he turned to the teaching of Hebrew as a livelihood. Emanuel Neumann described him as a typical Lithuanian *talmid hakham* (scholar).

Both men grew up in an environment where Hebrew was a spoken language and an instrument of culture. Ben-Gurion spoke Hebrew even before his migration to Palestine. During his first trip to Warsaw at the age of 18, he met Nahum Sokolow, the well-known writer and editor of the journal *Ha-Tsfirah*, and was dismayed to discover that the esteemed Sokolow could hardly speak Hebrew. All of Ben-Gurion's letters to his relatives were in Hebrew — a phenomenon quite unusual at the time. Silver also had a special relation to the language: in the Herzl club he founded in New York, the young members conducted their deliberations and presented their talks and lectures in Hebrew. This provided the occasion for the first clash between Abba Hillel Silver and representatives of the American Jewish establishment. Displeased with his demonstration of Jewish particularism, they called on him to change the language of the club to English. The young Silver refused, and this was the first expression of his dogged stubbornness and resolute will.

Yet despite almost identical beginnings, their migrations from Eastern

Europe went in different directions. At the age of 9, Abba Hillel Silver migrated to New York with his family. Ben-Gurion also left the Pale, immigrating to Palestine before his 20th birthday. Their personality and paths of action, views and beliefs were all molded by these voyages which were to have formative impact and be of fateful importance. There is a story that Silver's father had wished to migrate to Palestine rather than the United States. It is fascinating to speculate what course Silver's life might have taken had his father indeed realized his Zionist dream. But the fact is that Silver landed in New York in 1902 and his biography evolved as the result of that reality, just as Ben-Gurion's life was shaped by the centrality of Palestine.

The first of the salient differences between the two men was in their education. Like other leaders of the *yishuv* (the Jewish community in Palestine) such as Berl Katznelson, Yitzhak Ben-Zvi and Yitzhak Tabenkin, Ben-Gurion did not finish secondary school. Aside from a short stint as a law student at the University in Istanbul, terminated with the outbreak of World War I, Ben-Gurion never engaged in systematic studies. He was an autodidact par excellence. His education was eclectic, nourished by the intellectual fashions popular among *maskilic* (enlightened) young Jews in the Pale of Settlement. Ben-Gurion's Jewish traditional education was limited. It consisted of what he had learned up to age 15 in *heder* and the *bet ha-midrash*. From that time on, he did not return to religious studies. This was also when he stopped observing the *mitsvot*. He was engaged in reading modern Hebrew literature and the Hebrew press, and was especially influenced by Micha Yosef Berdyczewski, the spiritual father of the vitalist current in Zionism. To a lesser degree, the critical essays of Ahad Ha-Am also had an impact on his thinking. Classic Russian literature, then at its creative peak, was also a vital part of his general education. He admired Tolstoy, Dostoevsky and Chekhov. In Warsaw, he encountered nascent socialist Zionist circles, the early Poalei Zion. The Marxist paradigm was a powerful force in the intellectual world of Ben-Gurion's generation and social class. Even those who did not accept the Marxist world-view in its entirety tended to adopt some of its ideas and integrate them into their own basic *Weltanschauung*. Ben-Gurion embraced that ideology and fused it with his Zionist views: when he immigrated to Palestine he intended to help bring into being a Hebrew proletariat.

Silver tread a different path. His home was not under the spell of revolutionary ideas. Indeed, Vilnius in particular and Lithuania more generally were seized by revolutionary fervor at the time: this was the very cradle of the Bund, the center of Jewish and Russian revolutionary activity. But these currents did not penetrate the Silver home. The young Silver remained unaffected by secularization and alienation from religion which played a role in Ben-Gurion's maturation. Migration to the United States did not lead him to abandon religion. On the contrary: Silver's parental home was full of devotion to traditional Judaism and *Yiddishkait*. His love of Zion was part of his devotion to Jewish tradition — not, as in the case of Ben-Gurion, its antithesis.

Until the age of 18, Silver was a pupil at his father's Hebrew school, and then went on to Hebrew Union College, where he graduated in 1915. At the same time, he completed his studies at the University of Cincinnati. Silver's decision to study at Hebrew Union College was accidental. This college, where the German-Jewish influence was a dominant factor, offered to outstanding students from families who had immigrated from Eastern Europe scholarships and even the chance to study at the University of Cincinnati. It was one of those decisions that are sometimes taken almost inadvertently, unthinkingly — but which then prove fateful for one's entire life. His ordination as a Reform rabbi determined the frame for Silver's thinking on matters of ideology, world-view and social involvement. It also stamped the style of life for Silver's young family, the place they chose to live and source of income.

Silver's studies took him along a course of Americanization: he grew distant from the ways of living rooted in Yiddish culture characteristic of the masses of immigrants in New York at the time and he embraced an American Jewish identity, in the spirit of the cultural traditions of the German Jews. That identity was based on the fundamental ideals of American society, its credo of human liberty, the pursuit of happiness, individualism and a boundless faith in progress. Silver accepted the formulae prevalent at the time among Reform Jewry regarding the general humane ideals of Judaism. These formulae blurred the national character of Jewish identity. Yet in Silver's thinking, such notions were transformed: he believed that the realization of these lofty ideals depended precisely on maintaining a strong Jewish identity rather than assimilating to the majority society. Hebrew language and culture were key instruments in this enterprise of preservation of self. His Zionist thinking at that time was heavily influenced by Ahad Ha-Am, especially Ahad Ha-Am's ideas on the superior ethical quality that a Jewish spiritual-intellectual center in Palestine would need to embody and radiate as a beacon to the world. The Jewish spiritual center would nourish the Jews of the Diaspora with elevated spiritual content; that would assist them in preserving their identity as Jews. This was a brand of Zionism whose wellspring lay in the search for identity — and not in the quest for an answer to the problems of the Jewish masses.

Thus, already at this early stage in their development, it is possible to distinguish quite distinct patterns of belief and behavior. Ben-Gurion matured in a world where ideology and political involvement were an integral part of a person's identity. His joining the party Poalei Zion was, so to speak, part of his rites of passage. The ideology marked out the goal and the means to reach the goal. The party was the tool for implementation and realization of the ideology: the revolutionary collective was the carrier of the process of historical development. Politics was the supreme framework, all-embracing, containing within itself cultural, social and even economic activity. The collective revolutionary outlook and ethos were a characteristic feature marking the patterns of action and organization of the labor movement in Palestine and the *yishuv* more generally.

Silver, by contrast, rejected ideological fervor along with the Yiddish language, and distanced himself from party spirit. The emblems of Eastern European identity were supplanted by proper English, American middle-class attire and a belief in the American credo, based on individualistic Puritanism and the principles of the American Revolution. Silver interwove these American qualities with compatible universalist elements of Judaism and created a unique fabric of thought.

Ben-Gurion's migration to Palestine marked the beginning of his emergence into prominence as a gifted leader. The encounter with Palestine crushed leaders who had been raised on the soil of the Diaspora, spawning a new group of leaders for whom the enterprise of building Palestine took priority over all other interests of the Jewish people. Ben-Gurion was one of that new elite who took hold of the reins of power. His rise to leadership was not rapid, though already at the time of the Second Aliyah he drew attention to himself by his rhetorical and journalistic abilities and his political skill and savvy. Ben-Gurion became one of a number of outstanding personalities in the movement: Berl Katznelson, Yitzhak Tabenkin, Chaim Arlosoroff, Eliahu Golomb, along with an entire gallery of further personalities. This was a leadership elite that did not hesitate to curtail Ben-Gurion's freedom of action, and more than once obliged him to moderate his position or even to alter the public agenda he wished to set. Within the framework of that group of leaders, Ben-Gurion learned the secret of mutual dependence between a leader and his supporters. These men and women recognized and respected his special abilities. This is why his threat to resign was always an important tool in getting his way. On the other hand, without his comrades, who gave him not only public support but also their crucial backing in implementing the principal goals of the group, he was bereft of any real power.

Silver did not pass through the annealing crucible of membership in a leadership collective. The party as a membership organization founded on a set of clearly identifiable ideological tenets did not take hold in American political life. The two great political parties in the American arena were *ad hoc* coalitions welded together for the purpose of electoral campaigns.

They lacked the same degree of binding character and social cohesiveness characteristic of political parties in Europe. Their dominant thrust was social, cultural and community activity. In the first four decades of the century, rabbis played a leading role in Jewish community life in the United States. Silver's decision to become a rabbi reflected his understanding of the structure of power within American Jewry and his desire to find his niche within that structure. He became an outstanding and respected leader in his community. Thanks to his considerable gifts as a preacher and expositor of scripture, his position within that community was unassailable. But there was a price to be paid: Silver's power was limited in scope. Unlike Ben-Gurion, whose power base grew gradually to national prominence, Silver remained essentially a local leader. Moreover, Silver was not active in a framework that forced him to adapt to the pattern of "give and take" characteristic of a political system. He was accustomed to working and acting solo — there was nothing in his biography that had prepared him for another type of situation.

The Zionist ideas espoused by Ben-Gurion and Silver in the 1930s were at opposite poles. Ben-Gurion approached Zionism as Herzl did, adhering to the view that time was running out. His untiring struggle with the Mandate authorities in the 1930s to increase the number of certificates for immigration was waged in the face of the growing anxiety about the fate of German and Polish Jewry, two large Jewish communities endangered by an ever more powerful and virulent anti-Semitism. At the outset of that era, Ben-Gurion was extremely impressed by Arthur Wauchope, the "best of the high commissioners," as he dubbed him, and he rejected his fellow leaders' tendency to attribute demonic designs to the British. Ben-Gurion was very excited about the 1937 partition proposal of the Peel Commission, that for the very first time broached the idea of establishing an independent Jewish state in a part of Palestine. But bitter disappointment came on the heels of that short-lived euphoria: the British, on the eve of World War II, backed away from the idea of partition. Instead, the 1939 White Paper reflected a policy that was openly anti-Zionist, meant to freeze the *status quo* in Palestine and put a brake on the development of the Jewish national home there. Already in 1939, Ben-Gurion proclaimed war on the White Paper, and although there were ups and downs in his position regarding the British during World War II, one can discern a shift in his thinking from the issuance of the White Paper on. In order to find an alternative to relying on Great Britain, he gravitated toward the United States.

In contrast to Ben Gurion's admiration for Berdyczewski and Herzl in those years, Silver remained loyal to ideas that were influenced by the thinking of Ahad Ha-Am. Stephen Wise, the outstanding personality in American Zionist circles, also had a major impact on Silver's thought. Wise, who was also a Reform rabbi, championed a cultural conception of Zionism that gave considerable importance to the Zionist enterprise in Palestine, but did not view this as the be-all and end-all for the Jewish people. In Silver's thinking in the 1930s, continuation of Jewish existence in the Diaspora and the establishment of a spiritual center in Palestine were two parallel tasks of equal importance for the Jewish people. The question of "double loyalty" did not bother him: he felt wholeheartedly American. America was his national and concrete homeland — Zion was his spiritual homeland. Zion should be built slowly and gradually, according to the principle "not by might or by power but by the spirit." Even though he was shocked at the beginning of the 1930s by what he witnessed during a trip to Germany on the eve of the Nazi takeover of power, he was not moved by that same sense of impending urgency that spurred Ben-Gurion and his associates to act. During the 1930s, Silver was busily engaged in activities within a local community framework and in the state of Ohio, promoting reformed social legislation and support for the New Deal. He was not involved in activities on behalf of the Jews in Europe. His support of the boycott of German goods, deploring the Transfer Agreement attests to his incomprehension of the situation. Even when he became active in the work of the United Palestine Appeal (UPA) in the late 1930s, his approach did not change. He spoke against illegal immigration to Palestine at the Geneva Zionist congress held in 1939, calling on Zionists to preserve their loyalty to Great Britain, based on his assumption that the policies of the White Paper were only temporary measures. His loyalty to Britain reflected the sense of obligation felt by liberal circles in the United States to Britain as an imperiled democracy locked in battle with the totalitarian powers.

The blend of Silver's liberal outlook with the Zionism espoused by Ahad Ha-Am was not accidental; it reflected something deeply psychological deriving from his fundamental attitude to non-Jews. Typical for Jews from the Pale of Settlement was a powerful sense of suspicion toward non-Jews in general and the authorities in particular. This feature characterized the thinking of all leaders in the labor movement in Palestine. Indeed, some of them had more trust in the British, and some less; yet on the whole, distrust of the authorities remained deeply rooted. They always expected the worst. Thus, whenever the blow struck, they were never surprised, since deep in their hearts they knew that it must come. Although the Zionists always proclaimed that there existed an identity of interest between the British empire and Zionism, they never truly believed it. Ben-Gurion was aware that the Arabs enjoyed a strategic priority over the Jews in the Middle East. Thus, it was clear to him that a confrontation with Britain would be unavoidable, either due to a clash of common interests or because it was a non-Jewish authority, and could thus not be relied on.

By contrast, Silver, the proud product of a free and democratic society, was not influenced by the sentiments and attitudes of those who had been born and raised in the Pale. He felt he was a full citizen with equal rights and had nothing to fear from the authorities. So Silver tended to trust in the just cause of Britain, cradle of democracy, until proven otherwise. Yet it was that same high-minded sense of freedom that also guided him when he came to the conclusion that the authorities, British or American, were acting improperly when it came to the Jews. He never once felt constrained by any misgivings about "what the Gentiles might say." A fear of anti-Semitism, one of the factors underlying the cautious response of American Jewry to the plight of European Jews during the 1930s and early 1940s, did not cause him to hesitate. On the contrary: that was the reason for launching a frontal attack. Precisely because he was not apprehensive about any malice that might be forthcoming from the non-Jews or the authorities, he was able to mobilize the full force of the Jewish community and to cast the weight of American Jewry into the scales for promoting what he perceived as *the* Jewish task of the era: the establishment of a Jewish state. He conceived of American democracy as pluralistic, the expression of a dynamic balance between differing interest groups among its citizenry. He reasoned that the interests of the Jews as a pressure group were thus fully as legitimate as those of the Greeks or the Chinese — or any other nation the Americans ventured out to protect. He was convinced that Jewish and American interests were compatible. Not only was there no contradiction between them — they were the expression of the same set of underlying values. A democratic Jewish state was to be the smaller sister of the great American democracy. Its establishment in the Middle East would lead to stability in the region and would advance American influence there — a conception the leadership of the *yishuv* gave lip-service to but did not really believe in. Yet Abba Hillel Silver believed this with all his heart. That faith was a powerful stimulus for political action.

In the 1940s, these two leaders displayed a marked similarity in their character and basic understanding of the political scene. Both had personalities that were authoritarian, domineering. They did not flinch from confrontation. And it even seems that such confrontational situations drew out the very best in them. They were firm and resolute, courageous and not afraid to make difficult decisions if need be. They knew how to project a sense of total self-confidence that is the hallmark of great leaders — one that lifts them above the mass of mere mortals and inspires their flock to follow their lead in virtually blind allegiance. Their confidence was rooted in an internal recognition of the rightness of their chosen path, a self-assurance to the point where they are ready to take steps that would seem rash to others, even an invitation to disaster.

Both Silver and Ben-Gurion espoused the ideas of mass politics. While

Wise and Weizmann were outstanding in their ability to exercise a personal influence and adept at utilizing the network of personal connections which they developed with the American and British leadership, Ben-Gurion and Silver were not at their best in intimate meetings. In these situations, they tended to preach or make speeches. Their true arena was a rostrum before an audience of hundreds or thousands, using the media to appeal to public opinion. What caused what? Was it the decline in personal diplomacy that sparked a deterioration in the influence enjoyed by Wise and Weizmann? Or was it the ascendancy of Ben-Gurion and Silver to power that gave rise to the phenomenon of mass diplomacy? It appears that these factors were intertwined, expressing the growing involvement of the Jewish masses in the political processes taking place during the stormy decade of the 1940s. Silver and Ben-Gurion shared the sense of fierce indignation toward a treacherous Britain — perfidious Albion — and both recognized that a unique historical opportunity existed that should be seized to create a Jewish state. The courage of the one in leading the diplomatic campaign and the bravery of the other in reaching the necessary political and military decisions was what ultimately made possible the establishment of the State of Israel.

Nonetheless, there were enormous differences in the character of their leadership and the sources of their authority. As mentioned, Ben-Gurion developed by stages and degrees, gathering experience in jobs at various levels until he emerged on the scene as the unassailable leader of the young state of Israel. Initially he was a party leader, after that he served as secretary general of the Histadrut, then as the director of the Political Department of the Jewish Agency and the chair of the Zionist Executive. Only in 1947 was his unquestioned leadership position accepted in the *yishuv* and the Zionist movement. Silver, by contrast, appeared like a comet in parabolic orbit: active at the beginning of the 1920s, he later faded from view and ceased activity, returning to the stage of action in the UPA in 1936. Once again he returned to Cleveland and his post as rabbi. Only in 1943, after reports of the Holocaust began to filter in, did he enlist his full energies for Zionist activity, and this only after he had been requested to do so by Weizmann and others. A comet in politics has advantages and drawbacks. His rise to the summit did not embroil him in destructive ideological or personal struggles and he did not incur any obligations or engender any ill-will. The status of a comet provides a leader with a position of unshakable independence, and a threat to resign is far more powerful than any such threat coming from someone established within the system. But independence also has its price: just as he has no obligations to others, others owe nothing to him. He has no coterie of companions at his disposal whose job is to pave the rocky path for him and assist him in finessing the necessary compromises. Nor is he accustomed to work with such a group of supporters. As a result, any explosion in the system of personal relations is shattering, burgeoning into a total crisis.

Ben-Gurion began his career as an oppositionist in the Zionist Organization. Acting as a representative of the World Alliance of Poalei Zion, he and Berl Katznelson attended the London Conference (1920) as advocates of constructive socialism. They wished to prohibit the participation of private capital in the construction of Palestine, or at least to ban the purchase of land by private individuals. Both felt offended by the evident disdain shown them at the conference. During the 1920s, Ben-Gurion and his associates appeared as the opposition to the executive of the Zionist Organization, sometimes vehement in their demands, at times more moderate. The process of "domestication" of the oppositional revolutionary and his transformation into an adherent of the established position accompanied Ben-Gurion's political path through a series of posts. Hence, the man who threatened in 1930 to blow the British Empire out of the water became an admirer of Wauchope and one of the architects of cooperation with Britain, until the rift in 1939.

The path taken by Silver was just the opposite: he began his career as a man of the dominant political power and remained loyal to the Jewish-American establishment until 1943. Only then did he shake off his semblance of "responsibility" and become the "*sheigetz*" (rascal) of American politics. His readiness to revolt against the spiritual authority of Wise, and in particular to challenge the historical partnership of the Jews with the Roosevelt administration; his political instincts, manifested in his readiness to discard the old guidelines in the game of politics, setting down new rules in sophisticated maneuvering between the two great parties, exploiting the electoral strength of the Jews of New York — all transformed him overnight from a man of the establishment into one of the opposition.

Silver the oppositionist rose to the very apex of American Jewish leadership, but was isolated on that lonely peak of power. The established bureaucracy did not adjust to the revolutionary change and wished to bring about his downfall. It was here that the concomitant isolation of the comet worked against him. When Ben-Gurion took steps which many of his associates in the leadership ranks of the Mapai party were opposed to, he was able to rely on broad support from his associates and from the rank and file. He had always been able to appeal over the heads of his opponents to the grass roots of the party. Not Silver: the organizational framework he so brilliantly built was one of a pressure group, tending only toward forceful action on a *single* issue. He did not construct a political network that might back him on any and every question. Moreover, American Jews were not organized on the basis of direct electoral representation, but on a system of representation through intermediary organizations. The representatives constituted the establishment of the Zionist Organization. Because of this indirect representative system, Silver found himself unable to translate the broad popular support for him and his program into a political force. When a crisis raged, the Zionist establishment was forced to tolerate his leadership. But once the crisis ebbed, he was sent packing.

It is impossible to imagine Ben-Gurion's life without his public activity. All his adult life he lived, ate and breathed politics — this to such an extent that his non-public life was meager in content and minor in importance. It is enough to read the letters he wrote to his son, full of political insights, to understand how little he distinguished between the private and public spheres. Silver's life was quite a different story: it is possible to imagine Silver's life without his plunge into politics, without his digression from his role as a rabbi in Cleveland. He returned to it and to religious philosophy when he abandoned the arena of political activity. Silver found great satisfaction in his work as a teacher, the spiritual mentor of a congregation. The position reserved for him in the temple was both a political advantage and disadvantage. An advantage, because he did not have to compromise in order to protect his position in the world of politics — and a drawback, since it made it easy for him to retire when things were not to his liking. In Ben-Gurion's case, politics was a life-long profession; in Silver's, it was optional.

This distinction is bound up with their differing characters as leaders. Ben-Gurion was a "total" leader both in times of peace and construction and in times of war, on days both ordinary and earth-shaking. Silver, by contrast, was the type of leader that is summoned from his retreat, like de Gaulle from Colombey les deux Eglises, when the people faces a crisis. Once the crisis has passed, the need for this type of leadership also melts away. It is difficult to endure for very long the tension and strain that such a leader demands from his flock. For that reason, once the emergency is over, the two sides, as though by secret and subliminal agreement, part company and go their separate ways.

Ben-Gurion, an oppositionist who shaped the establishment, was enshrined in the memory of Israel as the dominant figure in the creation of the state. Whereas the historical memory of American Jewry has not done proper justice to the memory of Rabbi Silver, who more than any other succeeded in providing it with political power and a sense of self-esteem. During his lifetime, Silver was unable to make himself into a personality that was part of the mainstream of American Jewish life, nor did he achieve this after his death. Thus, the opaqueness of historical memory regarding his life and work was an inevitable product of the intrinsic nature of his mode of leadership.

Sources

David Ben Gurion, *Memoirs* (Hebrew), Vols. I-II, Tel Aviv, 1971–1972.

Aaron Berman, *Abba Hillel Silver: Zionism and the Rescue of the European Jews*, New York, 1979.

Bitzaron (Hebrew), Abba Hillel Silver Issue, vol. 48, No. 5, April 1963.

Zvi Ganin, *Truman, American Jewry and Israel*, New York, 1979.

Emanuel Neumann, *In the Arena: An Autobiographical Memoir*, New York, 1976, (Hebrew translation by G. Arioch) Jerusalem, 1977.

Noach Orion (Herzog), "The Leadership of Rabbi Abba Hillel Silver on the American Jewish Scene, 1938–1949" (Hebrew), Ph.D. dissertation, Tel Aviv, 1982.

Anita Shapira, *Berl, The Biography of a Socialist Zionist*, Cambridge, 1984.

Abba Hillel Silver, *In War and Peace: The Role of Jewish Palestine*, UPA, 1942.

————————————, *Vision and Victory: A Collection of Addresses, 1942–1948*, ZOA, 1949.

————————————, *The World Crisis and Jewish Survival*, R. R. Smith, 1941.

————————————, *Selected Sermons and Addresses*, World Publishing, 1967.

————————————, *In the Campaign for a Jewish State* (Hebrew), Jerusalem, 1968.

Shabtai Teveth, *The Zeal of David: The Life of David Ben-Gurion* (Hebrew), Vols. I-III, Tel Aviv/Jerusalem, 1976–1987.

Zion and America:
The Formative Visions of Abba Hillel Silver

Hasia R. Diner

"THE AMERICAN JEW fights under the Stars and Stripes. That is his flag," wrote Abba Hillel Silver in a 1942 pamphlet, *In War and Peace: The Role of Jewish Palestine*, while the

> Palestine Jew should be free to fight under the Star of David. That is his flag....
> America's war is our war, in a three-fold sense: ours because it is our country....
> American Jews have always known how loyally to serve their country.... It is
> our war, too, because the fundamental human ideals which are at stake...are of
> the very essence of the Jewish spiritual tradition.... It is also our war because
> our very survival is at stake.[1]

Addressing both American Jews and the larger American public, during several decades Silver framed the relationship between America and liberalism, Jewish life and Zionism, into a single, coherent statement. He hoped to convince American Jewry of its duty to participate unstintingly in the war effort while raising its collective consciousness regarding Zionism. At the same time he sought to prove to Americans that Jews shared a common vision and destiny with the United States, and that references to Jewishness and Zionism did not constitute a compromise with America.

In this brief passage Silver, the charismatic orator and Zionist political operative, known in the Jewish world and on the American scene as a brilliant speaker, powerful writer, and key figure in the movement to create an independent Jewish state, staked out his ground as American and Jew. In it Silver pulled together the core elements of his thought as he envisioned an America committed to "human ideals" which co-existed and grew out of Judaism. He eschewed accusations of disloyalty among those citizens who also may have identified with other lands and peoples. Silver envisioned the heroic American Jewish man prepared for combat under the Stars and Stripes marching together with the battle-ready Jewish man of Palestine

---

1   Abba Hillel Silver, *In War and Peace: The Role of Jewish Palestine*, New York, 1942, pp. 8–9.

beneath the Star of David. He proclaimed to the Jews of America that Zionism would enhance their personal dignity. They would be reinvigorated, actually rescued, by both fighters, the first who confirmed their place in a liberal America, the second whose right to national sovereignty informed Silver's lengthy Zionist career. Both were fighting for common ideals encapsulated in the American vision of liberalism.

To Silver the fate of American Jewry in the early twentieth century lay precisely in the twinned essences of Judaism and American democracy. Both stood in danger and both needed to be restored through Zionism and liberalism, potent weapons in the fight against the forces of reaction that came as much from within as from without. Both political movements offered solutions to the declining conditions of the Jewish people in America, and America itself. To the Jewish War Veterans, he said, in 1938, "Our refuge as Jews, is the God of Israel who neither slumbereth nor sleepeth and our refuge as Americans is the spirit and traditions of the Constitution of the American people."[2]

While rabbis, writers, educators, and others on the American Jewish scene were fashioning a rhetorical tradition based on similarities and parallels between American civic culture and Judaism in order to secure the status of the Jewish people in America, Silver, in the decades of his career leading up to the 1940s, developed an idiosyncratic formulation that encouraged Zionism in the name of liberal Americanism. He offered a rationale by which American Jews could embrace Zionism and liberate the Jewish community from a deep communal and spiritual crisis, just as he offered American society a rationale to resolve the contradictions between democratic ideals and realities that fell far off the mark. Both Zionism and liberalism constituted the means to a single end. For both America and for its Jews that hoped-for end involved the creation of an ideal, organic community that enhanced spiritual life and gave meaning to its members. Only internal communal democracy could foster this, a democracy that in Jewish life meant Zionism and in American society dovetailed with the early twentieth century liberal agenda. Jews in America needed to experience a spiritual regeneration by learning what lay at its core (presumably the role of the rabbi) and then freeing themselves from those abnormalities that had developed over time. America too, Silver intoned, had to come to terms with and recognize its democratic essence, and then behave according to the fundamentals of its creed, by restructuring national life. Political liberalism and Zionism both would make it possible to "be healed and made whole by becoming more

---

2   A. H. Silver, "Jews Don't have to Apologize! Let Us Not Permit Ourselves to Be Put on the Defensive," *The Jewish Veteran*, vol. 7, no. 1, October, 1938, pp. 6–7, 15.

truly and more intimately themselves and more at home with their own racial genius."[3]

Zionism functioned in the imagination and activities of Abba Hillel Silver as the potential catalyst for creativity and energy in American Jewry. Democracy would fuel a shift in the community away from philanthropy as the key organizing principle to the primacy of the will of the masses; from being based upon materialism to valuing spirituality; from domination by the monied elite to respecting the mandate of the majority. Zionism represented to Silver not just a political program for the rescue of the oppressed Jews of Europe, refugees originally from World War I and then the even more desperate refugees of World War II, but as a potent source for redirecting and restructuring American Jewish life, making possible a multiplicity of definitions of Jewishness. Thus, Silver the Jew considered American Jewry to be in need of fundamental reform that only Zionism could spark.

So too, Silver sought to redirect the values and institutions of America. As an activist in a series of progressive causes and as a prolific writer on a range of topics not specifically Jewish, but always Jewish by implication, he envisioned a future America where the overwhelming power of business would be diminished in favor of what he saw as the basic beneficence of the popular will. He envisioned a grassroots revulsion against, and rejection of, *laissez-faire* in favor of an organic definition of community and society that accepted the idea of social responsibility through the economic activism of an interventionist government. He chided America for its belief that unity came from cultural conformity and that racial and ethnic differences could not coexist within a common culture. He celebrated cultural pluralism and pointed out repeatedly the inconsistency of a society that practiced racism while claiming to be democratic. He spoke out for a radical restructuring of American institutions and values, although always within the context of liberal pluralism. At the 1934 annual meeting of the National Education Association, Silver told the assembled teachers, "If we are to work for a better social order, our children must be taught to know what is wrong with the existing social order....The model for emulation set before the growing child should not be the poor boy who by dint of work and thrift became rich, but the boy who by dint of cultivation of his character...became a valuable member of the community, a builder of the better social order."[4]

His vast corpus of speeches and articles churned out at dazzling speed indicates the merging of American and Jewish idioms in his thought. America as a society faced the danger that its democratic institutions were

---

3   A. H. Silver, *The World Crisis and Jewish Survival: A Group of Essays*, New York, 1941, pp. 47–48.

4   *New York Times*, February 27, 1934, p. 17.

being eclipsed by anti-democratic forces. Those institutions, and the values upon which they were designed, needed to be restructured along progressive lines. Likewise, American Jewry had distanced itself from the essentials of Judaism by its own internal foes of communal democracy. Silver saw the connections clearly. "Just as democracy and liberalism," he gloomily prophesied in 1941, "will perish unless they resume their offensive, so the Jewish people will be defeated and beaten into servitude unless they fling themselves resolutely into the fight with Amalek."[5]

In Silver's diction is reflected the fundamental integrity of Abba Hillel Silver the Zionist and Abba Hillel Silver the crusader for a democratic America. From the start of his rabbinate in the years of World War I until the mid-1940s, Silver staked out the common ground between Zionism and liberalism, Judaism and America. If Silver felt any conflict between these loyalties he never discussed them. Indeed, he moved effortlessly in the same article, the same paragraph, sometimes in the same sentence, from solving America's problems by means of an expanded democracy to solving Jewry's malaise by means of Zionism. That movement, he proclaimed in his single-most cited speech, the one delivered at New York's Biltmore Hotel at the Zionist Conference of May 1942, "is part of the historic struggle of men and nations for liberty, freedom and justice; without these Zionism has no meaning, purpose or hope."[6] He repeatedly used these same words to describe America's stake in the war, and more broadly, the ideal and meaning of the promise of American life.[7]

Silver viewed with alarm the condition of the Jews in America and the condition of America itself. Ever the activist, he energetically diagnosed their maladies and prescribed solutions for reform. Essentially, Silver believed that Zionism was the antidote to the low spiritual and cultural condition of the Jewish people in America, and that real democracy was the force that could save America from itself.[8] According to Silver, Zionism as a movement

---

5   Silver, *The World Crisis and Jewish Survival*, p. 46.

6   *New Palestine*, vol. 32, no. 14, May 15, 1942, p. 11.

7   See, for example, A. H. Silver, "What Alone Can Save Our Democratic Way of Life," in G. Paul Butler, *Best Sermons: 1944 Selection*, Chicago, 1944, pp. 275–282.

8   The literature on Progressivism shows that a variety of diverse movements for reform were considered, at the time and subsequently, to fit under the Progressive standard. Although all reformers agreed on some issues, Progressivism was as much a cultural as a political movement and can be characterized by an inordinately high level of physical and emotional energy expended on attacking the multiple problems attendant on a society undergoing a radical transformation to industrial and corporate capitalism. It depended greatly on public opinion and public activism and it emanated from and also generated an overweening sense of activism. For one attempt to characterize Progressivism, see Arthur S. Link and Richard L. McMCormick, *Progressivism*, Arlington Heights, Illinois, 1983.

to regenerate Jewish life, and efforts to strengthen democratic liberalism in the larger society developed from common roots, shared common concerns, and embodied common ideas.

Indeed the democracy that Silver held up as the goal for America to attain was in fact an American variant of the Jewish tradition. To Silver, the legacy of "propheticism" that he saw as a form of "protest" profoundly informed Judaism. That protest tradition, that could make life in America better for all of its citizens, not only had Jewish roots in a general sense, but in fact grew out of the soil of the land that Zionism sought to reclaim. Not a product of the Diaspora, the call for social justice and economic equality, like the other core elements of Judaism, "Legalism, Mysticism, and Nationalism," had been "proclaimed on the hills of Judea and in the cities of Samaria." The Jewish version of democratic America then had grown in tandem with a commitment to, and a rootedness in, a particular piece of land.[9]

During Silver's lifetime, but more so in the subsequent treatment of his career by historians, his Zionism has functioned as the central interpretive focus of his life, while his involvement as an American liberal has been shunted to the margins or even ignored. Abba Hillel Silver has been presented as a Zionist in a number of biographical accounts, particularly those that focus on his later years, after 1942, and his electrifying speech at the Biltmore Conference. Certainly during his lifetime journalists and American politicians treated him as the epitome of American Zionism itself, seeking him out when they needed a Zionist commentator, using him to embody the American Zionist ideology. Throughout the half century of his rabbinate, from the second decade of the twentieth century until his death in 1963, Abba Hillel Silver projected himself as the exemplar of American Zionism, and Jewish and general newspapers hailed him as one of — or often the — preeminent voice of that movement. Historians of Zionism as a world-wide undertaking, taking the cues from contemporary observers, have likewise turned to Silver as the paradigmatic example of an American Zionist.[10]

Yet historians, as well as sociologists and political scientists with a historical interest in the connection between Jews and liberal politics, have somehow failed to consider Silver when discussing the Jewish involvement with American Progressivism. Analyses of Jewish participation in American reform explore both the contributions of and Jewish roots of Louis Brandeis, Belle Moskowitz, Horace Kallen, Felix Frankfurter, or labor leaders such as

---

9   A. H. Silver, "A Consummation: Palestine and the Jewish Spirit," *New Palestine*, vol. 10, no. 4, January 22, 1926, pp. 78–79.

10 See, for example, Gideon Shimoni, *The Zionist Ideology*, Hanover, New Hampshire, 1995, p. 118.

David Dubinsky or Sidney Hillman. Silver's immersion in the liberal causes of his day and his voluminous writings on almost every aspect of the liberal movement in its broadest definition rarely merit inclusion.[11]

Scholars like Marc Raphael, heretofore the only one to tackle Silver's career in a full-length biography, as well as Henry Feingold, Michael Meyer, and others, have focused on Zionism as the key aspect of Silver's identity. While Raphael makes mention of some of Silver's Progressive involvements and provides ample documentation through primary sources of Silver's extensive activities on behalf of the liberal agenda, he interprets these American concerns independently of Silver's Zionism and activities for the Jewish people. Feingold, in an interpretive survey of American Jewry between the end of World War I and the end of World War II, and Meyer, in a comprehensive history of Reform Judaism, treat Silver only as a Zionist (with one other reference in Meyer's work to Silver as a defender of the rabbinate), while gliding over Silver's active efforts to expand American democracy, surely a key element in both the Reform agenda of the twentieth century and in the self-definition of American Jewry between the two world wars.[12] Thus the Silver who emerges in the scholarly and more popular literature is Silver the fiery Zionist leader, the eloquent crusader for a Jewish state. He has been presented primarily as a kind of single-minded devotee of a single cause, disembodied from his concerns about the American nation.

Certainly Zionism consumed the lion's share of Silver's energy and as America and American Jewry moved into the 1940s and became acutely aware of the international cataclysm of World War II, other concerns paled by comparison to his ceaseless labors for the rescue of European Jewry in the context of pressing for Jewish statehood in Palestine. But having granted the primacy of Zionism on Silver's agenda, understood against the backdrop of the exigencies of the rise of Nazism, World War II, and the consuming Holocaust, no understanding of Silver's political and cultural program would be complete without attention to his activities in behalf of a reformed America. Ultimately his vision of what an invigorated, meaningful democracy could do for America was infolded with his vision of what Zionism could do for American Jewry.

Silver remained an American in America long after the establishment of the independent Jewish state and he always claimed that the vast majority of

---

11 See, for example, Seymour Martin Lipset and Earl Raab, *Jews and the New American Scene*, Cambridge, 1995.

12 Marc Lee Raphael, *Abba Hillel Silver: A Profile in American Judaism*, New York, 1989; Henry Feingold, *A Time for Searching: Entering the Mainstream, 1920–1945*, Baltimore, 1992; Michael A. Meyer, *Response to Modernity: A History of the Reform Movement in Judaism*, New York, 1988.

American Jews would do likewise. Their lives, like his, would be lived out in America and as such his involvement in a whole range of reforms, including women's suffrage, unemployment compensation, the closed shop and the recognition of labor unions, free speech, as well as his discursive writing on the problems of racial discrimination, cultural pluralism, and materialism, all bore witness to his deep involvement with American society.[13]

Silver began his career in the rabbinate in 1915, in the heyday of the Progressive era, with a strong commitment to that movement. Like many Progressives of his age, he articulated strong youthful striving for spiritual fulfillment and constructed a career for himself dedicated to serving the betterment of society. Even as a neophyte rabbi in a town with a very small Jewish population, he boldly took on a number of causes that put him at odds with the community around him. He seemed unconcerned with the possibility that his outspoken advocacy of sometimes unpopular issues might cause discomfort within the Jewish community, or would stimulate hostility from the Gentile one. In 1917 when Silver occupied his first pulpit in Wheeling, West Virginia, Silver's congregation, the Eoff Street Temple (Congregation L'Shem Shamayim) had arranged with Wisconsin's Senator Robert La Follette to deliver a speech. A group, numbering over one hundred, irate "representative, patriotic American citizens of Wheeling," demanded that Silver rescind the invitation, because of the Senator's uncompromising pacifism on the eve of United States entry into the World War. Silver, physically facing the angry assembled throng, not only defended La Follette's right to vote his conscience in the Senate, but he chided the crowd: "Men of your like are the real menace to democracy; you fan your shallow patriotism into a flame of furious intolerance which consumes all the sanctities of a nation."[14]

Likewise he actively campaigned in behalf of women's suffrage, not a particularly popular cause in late-Victorian America. As in many states, West Virginia's suffrage activists formed a "flying squadron" of ten women and men who barnstormed the state speaking for the cause. Abba Hillel Silver joined them and used his already impressive oratorical skills for the Equal Suffrage Association.[15]

Like many Progressives, he jumped enthusiastically into the heady spirit of World War I, not for its jingoistic, narrowly patriotic appeal, but because of its promise of universal peace, democracy, and the promise of

---

13 Raphael, *Abba Hillel Silver*, pp. 18–20, 59–60; Harold P. Manson, "Abba Hillel Silver — An Appreciation," in *In the Time of Harvest: Essays in Honor of Abba Hillel Silver on the Occasion of His 70th Birthday*, Daniel Jeremy Silver, ed., New York, 1963, pp. 8–9.
14 Raphael, *Abba Hillel Silver*, pp. 6–7.
15 Ibid., pp. 18–19.

self-determination for colonized peoples. In one of his earliest public addresses in August 1917 he asserted that the war would "do away with reasons for war," would be the harbinger of "happiness and freedom to all mankind." Additionally, he projected a special role for Jewish young men in uniform who would, "fight for Judaism and humanity."[16]

Like many veterans of the Progressive movement, he spent much of the rest of his career lamenting the war's carnage, cynically noting the tremendous disparity between the lofty but ultimately unrealistic aims that the progressives had all committed themselves to, and the war's dreadful, long term implications that ultimately led the world to yet another war and brought the Jewish people to the brink of destruction. In sermons and articles, he connected a host of social and spiritual ills to the war. It unleashed the hysteria of anti-foreignism that was then translated into the Red Scare, widespread suppression of civil liberties, and immigration restriction.[17] It brought in its wake a new form of "neopaganism" which he believed threatened American families and the fundamental values of community responsibility.[18] "What kind of a world," he asked in 1944, "did we build for our children after the last war? A world of wild inflation, bloated prosperity, disastrous panics, prolonged depressions and appalling unemployment," he answered himself.[19] Misguided diplomats and crass nationalists had imposed an unworkable peace upon Germany, and as early as 1919 he predicted that "any beaten nation that feels embittered and abused thinks not of peace but of war and plans vengeance."[20] Isolationism too grew out of the first great war, and Silver saw the attempt of Americans to close the doors around themselves as a major factor leading to the tragedy of the second global war. Isolationism made it possible for Americans to sit back and let Nazism rise to power, strip the Jews of their rights, destroy their homes, communities, and lives. For Silver, then, as for many idealistic Americans, veterans of the Progressive era, World War I proved to be a sore disappointment that for decades was referred to as a moral lesson to be studied and as an example to be avoided.[21]

A huge body of historical scholarship has focused on the question of what happened to Progressivism after World War I. While the movement may have declined and drifted off in a number of directions, Silver continued to

---

16 Quoted in Ibid., p. 23.
17 See, for example, "The Red Terror and the White," in Daniel Jeremy Silver, *Gleanings of an Abundant Harvest*, New York, 1963, pp. 32–33.
18 Abba Hillel Silver, *Religion in a Changing World*, New York, 1931, p. 155.
19 Silver, "What Alone Can Save Our Democratic Way of Life," p. 276.
20 A. H. Silver, "Is the Treaty of Peace A "Peace Treaty?" Daniel Jeremy Silver, *Gleanings of an Abundant Harvest*, pp. 30–32.
21 For a brief discussion of this subject, see Link and McCormick, *Progressivism*, pp. 105–113.

press for a variety of reforms that he saw as potent antidotes to the lack of ideals, the crassness, and exclusivity which increasingly characterized American life. Finding the encrusted party system a deterrent to democracy, Silver and others supported the idea of a Progressive Party in the mid-1920s. In October 1924, the *New York Times* reported that Silver favored the creation of a liberal party, with Robert La Follette at its helm to challenge "the conservative elements within both the Republican and Democratic Parties," which he believed resembled one another and ought to merge into a single party of the status quo.[22] Political parties like other institutions, in Silver's judgement, should serve to advance progressive values, expand political participation, and foster democracy, rather than serve as market-places for the brokering of power, which he saw as the focus of the established parties. Thus, a key element in Silver's Progressive vision involved the notion that politics must include a commitment to ideals. Success devoid of larger, spiritual meaning, had no place in Silver's world view. Without popular participation and the voices of popular opinion, politics served no purpose.

In these and in a range of other liberal causes, Silver, committed himself, and by extension his congregation and the Jewish community, to remaking America by enhancing democracy. Racial discrimination, a theme he harked to repeatedly, defied democratic values because of its categorizations of citizens by race. A society in which some individuals were excluded from the democratic process by virtue of certain characteristics, skin color, religion, national origin, deviated from "true" American values and made impossible an organic community. All Americans suffered from such discrimination; all numbered among its victims. Typically in 1942 he expostulated in *The Nation's Schools*, "Those who discriminate against Negroes...are helping to undermine the morale and the loyalty of millions of our people. We cannot wage war upon the vicious racialism of the Third Reich abroad and at the same time tolerate it at home in our free country."[23]

He continuously castigated American society for its failure to live up to its own principles, and more importantly for causing an enduring division in society. At the 1940 meeting of the Southern Association of Colleges and Secondary Schools he again made the connection between anti-Semitism in Europe and racism in America, noting, "There was a race problem in the United States long before the Nazis intensified the Jewish race problem. There was a Negro problem, and there is a Negro problem in this country,

---

22 *New York Times*, October 29, 1924, p. 2.
23 A. H. Silver, "Morale Building in America," *The Nation's Schools*, vol. 29, no. 3, March 1942, p. 47.

American-made, not imported."[24] He repeatedly linked racism to imperialism, war, economic exploitation, and in more than one article and sermon commented, "The doctrine of racial superiority was used as a cover for the vicious motives of the last war. It has always been a blind for economic imperialism. The people of the South used it as an excuse for exploiting the colored man and for denying him his elementary human rights and his legitimate opportunities. The white man's burden becomes the black man's curse, and brown man's, and the yellowman's."[25] Racism divided America into groups, serving to "re-create here the crazy-quilt patterns of the Old World." In a racist society, he chided America to recognize, "the majority suffers as much from minority discrimination of the minority itself."[26]

Silver called for an American society liberated from racial categories not just because of his moral disgust with racism, but because of his larger conception of the civic good. When, according to Silver, public life essentialized differences, it undermined the American tradition, destroyed the possibility of a harmonious community life, robbed all Americans of the possibility of spiritual meaning in their lives, and as such carried with it the seeds of America's downfall.

Jews had a special stake in making sure that America eliminated racism and invidious distinctions from the public sphere. A society that by law recognized classes of citizens would ultimately be a society dangerous for Jews. It would be one that replicated the evils of Europe. "Those people...in our midst," he warned the Jewish War Veterans amidst the gloom of August 1939, "who would break up American life into hostile racial or religious groups, and who would persuade others to judge American citizens...on the basis of the race to which they belong...are the deadliest foes...of the American people." Opposing racial and religious discrimination offered "our one chance to keep our dear country free of the ravages of the hates, bitterness and conflicts which have disfigured the Old World."[27]

Issues of labor and capital and the need for state intervention likewise played a prominent part in Silver's views on society and the need to jump-start democracy. He wrote voluminously and acted directly to ease class disparities in America, by calling for the recognition of labor unions and by demanding that state governments in particular put in place legislation to

---

24 A. H. Silver, "Social and Religious Tolerance as Related to National Defense," *Southern Association Quarterly*, vol. 5, no. 2, May, 1941, p. 232.
25 A. H. Silver, "The Decline of the Individual," *Oberlin Alumni Magazine*, vol. 31, no. 2, November 1934, p. 41.
26 A. H. Silver, "Freedom for All or Freedom For None," *Highroad: A Journal for Youth*, vol. 2, no. 6, June 1943, p. 18.
27 A. H. Silver, "The American Ideal," *Jewish War Veteran*, vol. 9, nos. 1–2, September-October 1939, p. 3.

protect laborers from greedy employers and the vagaries of the economy. In 1928, already ensconced in his prestigious rabbinate at the affluent The Temple (Congregation Tifereth Israel) in Cleveland, Silver launched a campaign to bring unemployment insurance to the working people of Ohio. The effort began in the meeting rooms of The Temple, and during the eight years that it took the Ohio legislature to pass the bill to provide such compensation, Silver directed the effort and helped draft the legislation.[28] In the public discussion about the open shop, which he abhorred, and the closed shop, which he advocated, Silver took a decisive stand not only in favor of the latter as a way to foster trade unionism, but as a way of castigating American society for its endorsement of laissez-faire economics and the carte-blanche it had given business. In response to a movement by the National Association of Manufacturers, representing a number of large corporations for the "American" plan, that is the open shop, Silver declared in a 1920 sermon, "Some protagonists of the open shop have appropriated for their particular form of organization the name 'American.'.... I want to say at the outset that all this talk...is unmitigated balderdash and bunk, and particularly pernicious at this time...if the policy of an organization like the Bethlehem Company...is American, then I, for one, am at a loss to understand what 'American' stands for."[29]

By participating openly and demonstrably as rabbi and Jew in insurgent causes on the American scene, Silver asserted that he, and other Jews like himself, acted as Jews always had and therefore fulfilled an — perhaps, *the* — historic mission of the Jewish people. In 1932, Silver predicted

> The depression, if long continued, may intensify the economic discrimination against the Jew which have been going on apace of this country....The Jew will become more and more a social ferment in our land, participating more and more in those liberal movements which aim at a radical reconstruction of our economic life. In the process he will draw the fire of resentment and hate of all those forces in our national life which profit from a continuation of the status quo. This is as inevitable in America as it has been elsewhere.[30]

Yet, when historians have treated Silver as a force on the American scene, it has been primarily in the context of his anomalous political

---

28 Manson, "Abba Hillel Silver," p. 8; Theda Skocpol discusses briefly the movement for unemployment compensation in Ohio, with no mention of Silver, but still provides a context for understanding the issue. See, Theda Skocpol, *Protecting Soldiers and Mothers: The Political Origins of Social Policy in the United States*, Cambridge, 1992, pp. 299–302, 636–637.

29 A. H. Silver, "The Coming Industrial Struggle–The Open vs. The Closed Shop," in Daniel Jeremy Silver, *Gleanings of an Abundant Harvest*, p. 39.

30 A. H. Silver, "The Relation of the Depression to Cultural and Spiritual Values of American Jewry," *Jewish Education*, 1932, p. 49.

behavior after 1940 when he rejected Franklin Roosevelt's bid for re-election and supported instead Wendell Wilkie. He developed a close alliance on the national scene with the Republicans and in particular with Ohio's Senator Robert A. Taft. Silver has been contrasted with the other great American Zionist tactician of the interwar years, Stephen Wise, who remained a loyal Roosevelt supporter and ardent Democrat, while Silver, who actually never became a Republican, determined that Jews, and Zionists, would be better served planting a foot in both parties, rather than continuing their single-minded devotion to the Democratic party.[31]

This odd chapter in Silver's political life distracts historians from recognizing the connection between American liberalism and Zionism in his thinking. It has diverted attention from the intimate bond between his American political liberalism and his Zionism. Silver's commitment to a democratized America cannot be considered separate from his agenda as an American Jew, which in turn had everything to do with what Zionism meant to him. His rhetorical repertoire resonates with the connections, parallels and similarities between America as a democracy and the essence of Judaism. His language explicitly juxtaposes liberal Americanism with the essence of Judaism, just as it offers the same assessment of the inner ill-health of both. "Lincoln," wrote Silver in 1927,

> somehow reminds one of the ancient prophets of Israel....Lincoln may be likened to that first great emancipator of mankind — Moses....Both were the servants of men but not their slaves. Both served their people with supreme devotion and sacrificial loyalty, but neither submitted to the whims and weaknesses of the men whom they led. Both Moses and Lincoln remain the unsurpassed examples... of the triumph of man over nature, over heredity, over environment.[32]

His 1928 book, *The Democratic Impulse in Jewish History* presented unabashedly the idea that Judaism at its core constituted a popular religion, and therefore constituted democracy. "God," asserted Silver boldly, "had made an eternal covenant with the whole House of Israel, that Israel as a people should become His pledged servant and emissary." This development in the evolution of religion constituted a democratic revolution.

> For the first time in the history of mankind a whole people conceived of itself as having been consecrated into an everlasting priesthood and as having been commissioned to perform those functions which among other peoples were

---

31 Raphael, *Abba Hillel Silver*, p. 109.
32 A. H. Silver, "A Saint of Democracy," in Emanuel Hertz, ed., *Abraham Lincoln: The Tribute of the Synagogue*, New York, 1927, pp. 643–649.

relegated to a small official group of priests. Religion was never so democratized!

Israel's historic involvement with democracy constituted its fundamental principle,

> an astounding ideological fixation...woven by the racial psyche and forever after inseparable from the life and thought processes of the people — namely, that God had made an eternal covenant with the whole house of Israel, designating them His servant and emissary.[33]

The concept of democracy and its idealization in his thought integrates Silver the Zionist with Silver the American liberal. Strewn through hundreds of sermons and articles was his argument that Zionism and liberal democracy, expanded and strengthened, went together. Silver saw Zionism and democracy as both ends in themselves and as the means to something greater, something spiritual, that gave meaning to peoples lives. How did he weave together the two strands of his political and cultural essence, his Zionism and his commitment to an America that functioned democratically?

First, from the point of view of Silver's personal development, even in his youth he seems to have considered himself both Zionist and progressive, identities which he always kept deftly in balance. The story of his early involvement with the Dr. Herzl Zion Club is a preview of the seamlessness of his thought that would echo throughout his life. In 1904, the young Silver, age eleven, only two years in America, together with a number of other boys founded a Zionist club in memory of the Theodor Herzl. The young men conducted their meetings in Hebrew and met at the building of the Educational Alliance, a social settlement house on New York's Lower East Side that was dedicated to, among other goals, the Americanization of the newly arrived immigrants. Two members of the Educational Alliance's board of directors, the veterans of the Dr. Herzl Club recalled years later, came to pay an inspection visit and stopped in to see the Zionist youth group in action. The two, Henry Fleishman, director of the Educational Alliance, and educator Julia Richman, were appalled that the youngsters spoke anything other than English and that the word "Zion" appeared in the group's name.

According to the apocryphal story, Abba Hillel Silver (then still known by the name, Abraham), by this time age fifteen, stood up and challenged the adults. Any language that King David employed to write the Psalms or

---

33 A. H. Silver, *The Democratic Impulse in Jewish History*, New York, 1928, p. 23.

that Isaiah used to invoke images of universalism, brotherhood, and peace should surely be good enough for the Educational Alliance.[34] The story not only hints at the orator that would emerge and the charismatic presence that decades later would dominate pulpit and podium, but also how easily and early Zionism and the imagery of democratic liberalism were fused in Silver's mind. To the young Silver, the boys had the right to the language, name, and ideology of their choice, and had no reason to buckle under to the adult paranoia.

Throughout his career he castigated narrow definitions of Americanism that asserted that only a single mode of cultural expression served the larger principles of American culture. At the end of that same decade, in 1919, at the height of anti-immigrant hysteria, the Red Scare, and the public debate over "hyphenism," as a new rabbi he boldly addressed the City Club of Cleveland. "We do not," noted Silver, "lament the fact of our polychrome, variegated texture. We glory in the fact. And the solution offered by these exclusive Americans to restrict immigration and suppress foreign languages and newspapers is likewise a faulty thing."[35] A broad definition of American culture, a plasticity of national identity that allowed for multiple identities to co-exist, informed Silver's vision of America. Such a vision clearly made it possible to claim a stake in America and a stake in another land and a worldwide people in search of that land. Such a vision linked him to a broad swathe of Progressive era thinkers, Jane Addams, Florence Kelly, John Dewey, Horace Kallen, Randolph Bourne, all of whom in their own way called for some form of cultural pluralism and rejected the idea that to be an American, one's identity could not in part lay elsewhere as well.

As the young Silver faced the two Americanizers in the meeting room of the Educational Alliance, he managed in one sentence to link that which Jews specifically claimed as theirs, the Psalms and the prophecies of Isaiah, with concerns and needs that were not specifically Jewish, but universal for humanity in general. Offered as justification for the group's right to speak Hebrew and to keep the word "Zion" in its name, Silver's juvenile words reflected a lifelong sentiment that Zionism as an ideology embodied not the most narrow aspects of Jewish life, but its most universal and broad elements. Silver asserted that Zionism would not isolate the Jews outside the currents of modernity, but would be the force that would link them to the rest of the world. Only by achieving a normal status and manly self-respect in their own

---

34 Benjamin Friedman, "Dr. Herzl Zion Club," *Central Conference of American Rabbis Journal*, vol. 12, no. 3, October 1964, pp. 25–26.
35 A. H. Silver, *The Immigrant vs. The Foreigner: Address Given before the City Club, Cleveland, Ohio, December 13, 1919*.

homeland could Jews enter the mainstream of the modern world. Silver's mythic Zion, like that of the prophets he repeatedly invoked, would be "the spiritual capital of a regenerated humanity." Not exclusively for the cultural benefit of the Jews, Silver, invoking Isaiah and Micah, prophesied, "The peoples of the earth will flow unto it to receive instruction in the highest laws of justice and world peace." The reconstituted Jewish people in their homeland would "push on to the frontiers of the new world — the world of internationalism of economic freedom, of brotherhood and peace."[36]

So fundamentally did this element of Zionism pervade his thought that he reserved his most heated political venom in the 1930s and 1940s for those Jews, many of whom came from the same class and the same ideological orientation as his critics that day at the Educational Alliance, who claimed that Zionists threaten the political status of the Jews in America because they articulated a provincial, parochial, narrow group-based agenda that called into question the loyalty of American Jews. Silver rejected both their definition of America and their definition of Jewishness in favor of a liberal and Zionist one. Jews had the right, as Jews and as Americans, to identify with whatever political and cultural modes of self-expression they desired. No group in the community had the right to appoint themselves gate keeper and determine which positions could be heard and which positions should be silenced.

The commingling of Zionism and democratic liberalism involved in essence a negative assessment of the status quo in both the Jewish and American worlds. Both lacked essential communal coherence and unity because both had strayed from their essentially democratic natures. Separated from their democratic roots, they would be unable to achieve their intended purpose: giving meaning to peoples' lives in the context of a living and organic community life. In part both had been stripped of their democratic cores because they had fallen into the hands of a small coterie of the elite who opposed democracy. Both had become the exclusive domains of a small band of the wealthy, who in no way represented the core traditions of either worlds and who stymied the prospects for democracy. Zionism and liberalism offered tools to opposing these elites by regenerating community life through the invigoration of democracy, as expressed through the will of "the people." By then living in a reborn, redemocratized America or Jewish community, individuals, almost always universalized through male imagery, could finally achieve wholeness, normalcy, and then go on to create new, but authentic, cultures.

36 A. H. Silver, "Herzl and Jewish Messianism: Nationalism as a Means to a Greater Goal," in Meyer W. Weisgal, ed., *Theodor Herzl: A Memorial*, New York, 1929, pp. 254–256.

For Silver the American liberal, American democracy constantly faced threats and challenges, less from the outside in a military sense, but more importantly from the inside. Those challenges came primarily from the right, from those who articulated narrow, racially, ethnically, and religiously specific definitions of American culture and who therefore excluded millions from inclusion in civic life. Particularly during the years leading up to and culminating in America's entry into World War II, Silver spoke and wrote for general American audiences about the dangers America faced from racism, class antagonism, and other reactionary realities which undermined democracy. The ideas that he had articulated throughout his career emerged particularly sharply and clearly in these years as he lectured to community groups or wrote for a wide array of American publications about the need to remake America. "Democracy," he intoned to a radio audience in 1941 on the Columbia Broadcasting System's "The Church on the Air,"

> cannot long survive widespread and prolonged economic suffering. All dictatorships have risen to power upon the economic miseries of the people. A generation of young men and women denied the opportunity to work and to build careers, consigned to demoralizing idleness...is the dictator's workshop.

Silver's liberal America valued "the importance of the individual," to mitigate racial and religious distinctions in law and public life, "government by consent and not by constraint," relying as such on "voluntary enterprises...experimentation and step by step...evolutionary processes of trial and error," and finally, "the grace of tolerance." Americans, Silver reminded his listeners, "are a composite people."[37]

Certain key ideas informed Silver's liberal vision for America and for Jewry and justified democracy and Zionism. In both worlds, he believed, enlightened individuals could undo the wrongs of the present by turning to the past for inspiration, and looking to the future for new modes of expression. The will of the masses should, he believed, outweigh the resources of the wealthy. Silver's thought as an American incorporated key ideas that dominated the liberal agenda of the twentieth century. He believed that industrial capitalism could be made humane if those who had money had to share power with those who did not. He believed that optimism and a "can do" attitude about the future not only made sense, but without it, democracy had no prospect for survival. Unity rather than

---

37 A. H. Silver, "Preserving the Genius of Americanism," *Current Religious Thought*, vol. 1, no. 3, March 1941, p. 22.

divisiveness, creativity rather than stasis, constituted the essential elements of that democratic prospect. The ills America suffered from, its racialism, its hardening class divisions, its cultural superficiality, its materialism, all could be addressed by a spiritual renewal that only democratization could bring about. That renewal, Silver asserted in a ceaseless stream of sermons many delivered from the pulpit of the Temple to overflow crowds — Jewish and Gentile — every Sunday morning over the course of decades, would come about by first an American recognition of its own failings and then by a systematic reform from within. America could redo itself. It did not have to remain in its present condition.

American Jewry, as well, did not have to accept its present anemic condition as the inevitable future. For Silver the Zionist, American Jewry faced deep threats, less from the outside in the sense of anti-Semitism than from the inside. The nexus between Silver the Jew and Silver the American indeed can be drawn around the similarities between his rhetoric on liberal democracy and his rhetoric on Zionism. These two forces paralleled each other as both would provide the antidote to the low, and indeed declining, cultural state of their two constituencies. Zionism in essence would do for American Judaism what an invigoration of democracy would do for American life. Just as America needed to be remade and redemocratized to fulfill its mission and survive (because without the former, it could not expect the latter), so too Judaism needed Zionism in order to actualize its destiny and therefore continue into the future.

Silver assumed that most of the same ills that infected America also played havoc in its Jewish life. He wrote and spoke about the lack of unity among American Jews as a strategic political problem as well as a source of spiritual malaise. He believed that the division of American Jews into a small elite of wealthy philanthropists who determined the community agenda not only spelled disaster for projects — namely, Palestine — which they disapproved of, but diverted the community from Judaism's historic commitment to social justice. American Jews had sunk to a low level of spirituality, measured by the lack of religious intensity and by the absence of a strong interest in education. Their cultural creativity had fallen also to an all-time low, mostly because of the governance of the community by the rich, rather than by the popular will.

Silver the Zionist meshed with Silver the Reform rabbi. By proposing Zionism as the solution to the doldrums of American Jewry he explicitly and implicitly indicted the Reform movement for not being the force that might have created a spiritual and communal renaissance. "Reform Judaism," he lambasted his colleagues in the rabbinate at the 1942 meeting of the CCAR, "has not only failed to make progress in recent years, but it has actually retrogressed." Reform as an idea had much to recommend it at the time of its inception, Silver the committed Reform rabbi pronounced in a pointed history of his movement. Its "pioneer reformers and their disciples after them were good and loyal Jews." But, "they were too zealous to 'modernize' Judaism, and too self-conscious about modernity." They evince "a premature confidence that mankind was rapidly approaching the era of a universal faith," and "failed to note the dangerous shoals of nineteenth century nationalism."[38]

Silver knew what motivated his congregants and those of most Reform temples. American Jewry in the pre-war decades divided quite neatly along class lines and Reform, by and large, attracted the well-off among them. Anxious to articulate for themselves a Judaism that fit their bourgeois class status and their desire for inclusion in the American mainstream, they opted for decorum, respectability, and the veneer of rationalism. For this class, ironically, the one that paid his handsome salary, he expressed contempt. He saw them as the source of the continuing dissipation of that which constituted Judaism and as the reason for Reform's increasingly minimal commitment to tradition. As they grew "richer...the less need they had for religion. The upper classes which succeeded in reaching, if not the center, then at least the periphery of the non-Jewish world, were most supercilious in their attitude towards Judaism. When men are prosperous they find it easy to dispense with God — especially with a Jewish God."[39]

Silver spent much of his Zionist career attacking these very wealthy individuals, whom he castigated for leading the community along the lines of philanthropy, which was undemocratic in its nature, and cultural accommodation, which had stripped Judaism of its vitality and authenticity. Described by Silver as having "Bourbon mentalities,"[40] this group happened in large measure to be members of Reform congregations. His controversy with Louis Marshall, a well-known non-Zionist, long associated with New York's Reform Temple Emanu-El, over communal funds proved a case in point. Marshall and the Joint Distribution Committee (JDC) which he led in the 1920s had directed most communal relief monies to help the Jews in Central and Eastern Europe to rebuild there in the devastating aftermath of World War I. The JDC, Silver wrote to Marshall in a public letter that appeared in the *New Palestine*, should not be furthering Jewish accommodation to the hostile environment of Russia. The money should be used to build up the possibilities of the *Yishuv*, the Jewish community in

---

38 Reprinted in *Vision and Victory: A Collection of Addresses by Dr. Abba Hillel Silver, 1942–1948*, New York, 1949, pp. 204, 206.

39 Silver, *The World Crisis and Jewish Survival*, p. 56.

40 Quoted in Melvin Urofsky, *American Zionism: From Herzl to the Holocaust*, Garden City, New York, 1975, p. 426.

Palestine, and make it possible for increasing numbers of Jews to situate themselves in their own homeland. "What then," he asked Marshall, "is to become of Palestine," if the small coterie of philanthropists who ruled the community without any kind of popular mandate decided that Zionism put them in an uncomfortable position vis-à-vis their American, Gentile neighbors?"[41]

The unfolding of world events in the decades after his rhetorical challenge to Marshall, Silver believed, proved him right. Millions of dollars collected from Jews in America for the reconstruction of eastern European Jewry ended up wasted as the Jews of those lands found themselves by the end of the 1930s and into the 1940s victims of yet another, more cataclysmic war. The philanthropists, Silver shouted, had "lacked the vision" to face the truth and use the money for Palestine after the Balfour Declaration when creating massive settlements in the Jewish homeland had been a possible, real solution. American Jews foolishly had chosen to

> listen to their omniscient and infallible philanthropic mentors who counselled them to give all aid to the Jewries of Eastern and Central Europe, but only a pittance to that visionary project of impractical idealists in Palestine. One must be realistic, they argued — and what greater realist in the world is there than a successful Jewish banker or broker, and who can question his unerring judgment?[42]

His charge against community by philanthropy, and the obvious attack on the monied elite of the community, provided one of the most consistent elements in Silver's career as a Zionist, and echoed his critique of business leadership and class divisiveness in his liberal, American rhetoric.[43] Such community control violated principles of democracy, based as it was on the right of the wealthy to determine the course of society, rather than the right of the many for self-determination. Those wealthy individuals who, in the larger American society opposed movements for economic justice and exacerbated class tensions, in the Jewish community caused almost everything Silver abhorred. They infected American Jewry with "specific 'Galut' maladies ...timidity, escapism...dodging one's own shadow, protective disassociation from other Jews."[44]

---

41 *New Palestine*, Letters, October 29, 1925, November 6, 1925.
42 A. H. Silver, "The Cause of Zion Must Not Be Minimized," *New Palestine*, January 3, 1941, p. 5.
43 David Shpiro, *From Philanthropy to Activism: The Political Transformation of American Zionism in the Holocaust Years, 1933–1945*, Oxford, 1994, p. xxviii.
44 A. H. Silver, "In War and Peace," *New Palestine*, vol. 32, no. 9, January 23, 1942, p. 6.

But, Silver's disappointment with Reform as a solution to the larger cultural problems of American Jewry went beyond his passionate disagreement with the wealthy opponents of Zionism within its ranks. Reform, he asserted, had in its classical nineteenth century vision of itself, excluded and destroyed the concept of community, a prerequisite, by Silver's reckoning, for a healthy, Jewish life. Just as he asserted that America needed to come to a new, restored concept of a total community life, so too Judaism, had never in its traditional formulation, been a narrow religious entity, but one in which the everyday life of its people and its rites and rituals, literally grounded in a national homeland, had been fused into a single, coherent culture. At the 1935 meeting of the Central Conference of American Rabbis he exhorted his fellow Reform rabbis, many of whom still adhered to a strict constructionism of Judaism as religion, that "It is the total program of Jewish life and destiny which the religious leaders of our people should stress today — the religious and moral values, the universal concepts, the mandate of mission, as well as the Jewish people itself, and all its national aspirations."[45] When it came to the Reform movement's limited definition of what constituted Jewishness, he could be prickly and nasty. As early as 1916, the brand new rabbi had the temerity to get up at a CCAR symposium and castigate his elders by condemning the "religious aristocrats and theologic Know-Nothings," who oppose "all movements in Jewish life which do not directly and immediately emanate from the temple or synagogue."[46] Sterile, decorous ritual did not provide for meaningful community life nor did it provide American Jews with an inspiration for group identity.

The Reform movement, which had nurtured Silver as a young man, ordained him, provided him with a livelihood and platform from which to launch a national and international career, disappointed him. "One of the great values of a ritual," noted Silver at a CCAR debate over revision of the prayer book, "is its unbroken continuity."[47] That continuity and connectedness to the past obviously had been an issue of contention for Reform throughout its history, and its severing of Judaism from its national roots, constituted for Silver, Reform's failure. "Let's face facts. We are a people. We are recognized as such by the world. We are a religion. our people has always been completely identified with its faith.... I recall the statement of Rabbis: "Israel and his faith and his God are one," expostulated Silver in 1920 in a key essay, "Why I am a Zionist."

Herein lies the key to Silver's critique of Reform, and by extension his critique of American Jewish life and the cultural context of his Zionism.

---

45 Central Conference of American Rabbis (CCAR), Yearbook, vol. 45, 1935, p. 342.
46 CCAR, Yearbook, vol. 27, 1916, p. 235.
47 CCAR, Yearbook, vol. 40, 1929, p. 138.

Zionism provided *the* only way of reconciling all elements of Jewish culture into a single program.[48] Only Zionism could reconcile American Jews into a mass, popular, united front that did not squeeze Jewishness into a narrow definition. At a gala celebration to mark the eleventh anniversary of the Balfour Declaration, he waxed eloquent about the power of Zionism to unify the American Jewish people. "The Jews of America have finally discovered a common denominator, a common basis for cooperation — Palestine. You tell me what you do for Palestine," he pointed to the audience assembled at the Hotel Astor. "I point to what Palestine is doing for us here.... The elementary giving of charity...is something, but nothing is able to draw us together except Palestine and Palestine is doing it." Palestine, and Zionism alone, "can make whole and bring East and West, North and South into an *Agudah Echad*, one consecrated and devoted land of faithful men planning for the future and building the great day which is yet to come."[49]

The passion of Silver's Zionism matched his cynicism about the ability of Reform, and indeed the other denominations of American Judaism, to provide for a meaningful, popularly-based, Jewish existence in America. He lamented the fact that the "essential work of the liberal synagogue" had fallen into the hands of "women and ecclesiastics," evidence of Judaism's anemia.[50] On the other hand, he posited in Zionism the power to rejuvenate Jewish life, to give Jews, "a strengthening of self-confidence and a reaffirmation of faith."[51] It, not the range of American Jewish institutions, would provide a way of "rediscovering that ancient authentic voice and mood that was ours."[52]

If in Silver's vision Zionism provided the solution to the low spiritual and communal level of Jewish life in America, in the abstract, then those women and men who physically engaged in the rebuilding of Palestine, served a special role, from afar, in the rebuilding of American Jewry as well. They, the Jews of "Palestine are our chosen vanguard." They, who have "been carrying on the hard and sacrificial labor of land and national building" give American Jewry "a courage and a dignity which might well fill us with deep and justifiable pride."[53] Zionism could provide American Jews with a sense of common cause and common culture; a focus for idealism and a vision of the future. His imagery of the Jewish settlements in Palestine underscored the

---

48 A. H. Silver, "Why I am a Zionist," in Daniel Jeremy Silver, *Gleanings of an Abundant Harvest*, pp. 32–36.
49 *New Palestine*, vol. 15, no. 12, November 9, 1928, p. 374.
50 Alan Silverstein, *Alternatives to Assimilation: The Response of Reform Judaism to American Culture, 1840–1930*, Hanover, New Hampshire, 1994, p. 162.
51 *New Palestine*, vol. 27, no. 20, May 28, 1937, p. 1.
52 *New York Times*, April 27, 1926, p. 8.
53 *New Palestine*, September 23, 1938, p. 3.

metaphors of progress and optimism, designed to instill in American Jews the sense of being part of the heroes of the future rather than the victims of the past. Silver sacralized the efforts of the *Yishuv* as hastening the spiritual revival of their American co-religionists. As he described the opening of the Hebrew University in 1925, Silver soared in telling how the Jews of Palestine had not only created a modern institution of higher learning, but they had literally and figuratively been present when "the doors of the Third Temple are opening wide. The *Schechinah* returns to her home.... A hundred waste fields we tended. The thorn and the thistle were ours. Flowers and fruits others claimed. We shall now tend our own field."[54] He hoped that by showing the Jews of America portraits of life in Palestine, he would instill in them a notion of Jewish agency in the world. Palestine, he wrote in 1927, was "affording the Jew who has carried the burden of prophecy through the ages, an opportunity to express his social idealism in concrete, human institutions, in law and in national mores, in giving his visions of justice and equality a locale for materialization."[55]

American Jews had a great deal to gain from the labors of their sisters and brothers in the *Yishuv*. The images of these pioneers laboring under adversity would provide Jews in the relative comfort of America with a unifying cause, one which would transcend the internal fissures over religious practice, political orientation, economic class. It would liberate them from the "few timid, cowardly, so-called Jews," who pervert Jewish life by suppressing the will of the majority.[56] Indeed the base of popular support in America for Zionism, particularly that wing of the Zionist movement that emphasized settlement of the land as opposed to philanthropy for health care or education, came from the bottom up. The more ordinary rank-and-file Jews of America of relatively recent eastern European origins responded to the Zionist message more passionately than did the more affluent of longer American vintage. The American Jews who may have been most moved by Silver's message, swelling the ranks of Zionist organizations, came from precisely those classes of the community who had been outside the philanthropic Reform-oriented elite circles that Silver served as rabbi, but whom Silver never hesitated to castigate. Silver wrote for American Jewry a Zionist prescription in order to cure its maladies. Unity to replace disorganization; the voice and will of the people as the closest approximation of democracy to push aside the rule of the affluent givers who held the purse strings.

---

54 *New Palestine*, vol. 8, no. 13, March 27, 1925, p. 335.
55 Quoted in Frances N. Wolpaw, "A Rhetorical Analysis of Doctor Abba Hillel Silver's Speaking for Zionism," unpublished Ph.D. dissertation, Case Western Reserve University, 1968, p. 242.
56 Daniel Jeremy Silver, *Gleanings of an Abundant Harvest*, p. 35.

Silver offered yet another analysis of American Jewry's complex problems and again Zionism, its therapy. The Jews of America suffered from "defeatism" and "all too frequently...accept our enemies'" view of our "value as creative human beings."[57] This theme ran through Silver's rhetoric particularly in the late 1930s and early 1940s. Echoing a dominant motif in Zionist rhetoric that saw Diaspora Jews as fundamentally abnormal people by virtue of their statelessness and the psychological anomaly of having to always be in and of two peoples, Silver hit hard on the theme that only Zionism, buttressed by the stirring portraits of Jews who created, overcame their abnormality, grew not only crops but a living Jewish culture, could provide American Jews, denizens of the Diaspora, with a powerful counterimage. Either because of their relative prosperity and comfort, one explanation for why American Jewry functioned at so low a level of cultural creativity,[58] or because of the heightening of anti-Semitism both at home and abroad,[59] the energy and verve of *halutziut* (pioneers) and the imperative of rescue of European Jewry into a sovereign Jewish state alone could provide an emotional solution to Jewish abnormality. "Customarily we Jews," opined Silver in 1937 in an aptly entitled speech "Jewish People Cannot Be Intimidated,"

> are prone to accept the lowest estimates which people and our foes place upon us and upon our abilities. We have been indicted to accept the world's estimate about our lack of pioneering interest and pioneering abilities.[60]

By identifying with Zionism, by acting politically as Zionists, American Jews, sitting in their homes in the United States, could vicariously get their hands into the soil of the land of Israel and mythically derive self-respect. Although they might never — indeed would never in actuality — drain a swamp themselves, a reinvigorated American Jewry could get all the personal satisfaction of having done so by developing a bond with Zionism. Over and over again Silver exhorted the Jews' enemies and more importantly the Jews of America themselves who had internalized negative self-images, to turn their eyes to the *Yishuv*.

> To such a land, neglected for centuries by Arab and Turk, shot through with malaria and trachoma, these pioneers came and brought healing and redemption. They drained the marshes. They cleared the swamps. They

---

57 *New Palestine*, vol. 28, no. 2, January 14, 1938, p. 2; *New Palestine*, vol. 28, no. 4, January 28, 1938, p. 6; *New York Times*, March 24, 1938, p. 8.
58 *New Palestine*, September 23, 1938, p. 3.
59 *New Palestine*, vol. 27, July 12, 1937, p. 11.
60 Ibid.

introduced sanitation. They revived agriculture. They built orchards and gardens.... They dotted the plains of Sharon and Jezreel with settlements and villages."[61]

Not accidentally Silver the Zionist merged with Silver the product of the era of American Progressivism as he portrayed the heroic women, and mostly men, of the *Yishuv* who "cleared the jungles."[62]

He connected his Zionism here with his liberal Americanism not only by celebrating the progress that Zionists, vicariously through their support, and the pioneers by their actual efforts, had brought to the physical environment. He also basked in the assistance that they had rendered to the wasteland's inhabitants, the Arabs. The *halutzim* brought modernity to "a small backward oriental province...transformed into a progressive country."[63] The Arab population, mostly impoverished workers, according to Silver, had long suffered from victimization by their own elite, the *effendis* and absentee landowners. But, with "the coming of Zionism," they started to experience prosperity and progress. "The Jews have brought a large measure of prosperity to the country in which the Arab fully shares. The wages and standard of living of the Arab workingman have risen as a result of the coming of new industry and Jewish workingmen."[64] Once again, liberalism and Zionism rolled into a single entity; once again a society cruelly divided by class and mired in backwardness, experienced the power of progress, this time, though, in the calloused hands of Jewish pioneers, who labored in the swamps and fields not just for themselves, but for others, Palestinian Arabs and Jews in the far flung diaspora, at the same time.[65]

The heroism, creativity, altruism, and high self-esteem of Zionism would directly benefit the Jews of America. American Jewry could not rely upon itself and needed to turn elsewhere, Palestine,[66] for inspiration and cultural identity. European Jewry could no longer offer American Jewry spiritual meaning. Palestine alone could foster the regeneration of American Jewry. Silver declaimed:

> If one wishes to see the miracle and the mystery which is Israel, let him go to Palestine...and watch...the undefeated strength, the overarching confidence,

61 *New Palestine*, vol. 28, March 25, 1938, p. 5.
62 Wolpaw, "A Rhetorical Analysis," p. 253.
63 *New Palestine*, vol. 13, no. 8, September 16, 1927, p. 218.
64 Wolpaw, "A Rhetorical Analysis," p. 106.
65 Silver came close before the riots of 1929 to embracing the idea of a binational state. See Raphael Medoff, "American Zionist Leaders and the Palestinian Arabs, 1898–1948," unpublished Ph.D. dissertation, Yeshiva University, 1991, p. 150.
66 A. H. Silver, "The Changing and the Changeless," in Abba Hillel Silver, *Vision and Victory: A Collection of Addresses by Dr. Abba Hillel Silver*, New York, 1949, pp. 196–207.

the superb zeal and energy, the social vision and the personal idealism which....common folk, transfigured by an ideal, can achieve...not only...[for] our people...but [for] humanity itself.[67]

Belief in a common humanity, "a fairer and nobler way of life,"[68] "a land in which there is room for all," and where "the progress and well-being of any one group need not be purchased...at the expense of any other"[69] could have referred to both his democratic vision for liberalized America and that of a future, sovereign Jewish state in Palestine. Silver's reconstituted Zion resembled his redemocratized America. The idealism that the Jewish homeland would bring to the Jews of America and the revolutionary impact it would have on their community life, replicated perfectly the outlines of a reformed America. The fusion of Zionism and of democratic Americanism allowed him to advocate for two lands and two peoples, symbolized by those two soldiers, fused into one indistinguishable symbol, ready to sacrifice under their two flags.

67 Silver, *The World Crisis and Jewish Survival*, p. 49.
68 Silver, "The Changing and the Changeless," p. 196.
69 Silver, *The World Crisis and Jewish Survival*, p. 193.

Between Ideal and Reality:
Abba Hillel Silver's Zionist Vision

Arthur A. Goren*

"Vision coupled with a cold realism and a hard discipline."
Abba Hillel Silver, On *halutziut*, from a manuscript com-
memorating Joseph Trumpeldor[1]

"VISION" LIKE "MISSION" is a loaded word. Its meanings run the gamut
from the divine to the mundane. It resonates with the notion of an ideal
time and place. The vision of the prophets with its messianic promise of the
kingdom of God comes to mind. In this sense, it has long been a staple of the
preacher's rhetorical arsenal, particularly the Reform preacher, and it has
gone hand-in-hand with its twin dogma, Israel's mission to the Gentiles.
This was no less true in the case of Abba Hillel Silver. However, as few
others of his colleagues were capable of doing, he expounded upon the
prophetic texts with scholarly erudition and salvaged them, one might say,
from the long-held proprietorship of the Classical Reformers. In 1928 he
wrote (he had been saying this for some time): "Deutero-Isaiah, who of all
Jews most eloquently vocalized the missionary faith of Israel was, of all Jews,
the most nationalistic and Palestinian.... Universalism and nationalism
rightly conceived are never antithetical."[2] Good Reform rabbi and passionate Zionist that he was, he exhorted his listeners to follow the prophetic
teachings and called upon all Israel to take part in the Jewish national
revival. The two, he insisted, were inseparable; they constituted the core of
Judaism and formed the essence of the religious vision he offered his
listeners.

"Vision" also has a more mundane usage. In this sense it signifies unusual
discernment and foresight that combines realism with sound reasoning and

* I am greatly beholden to Arthur Kiron for his research assistance and especially for scouring
  the Silver microfilms at a time they were beyond my reach and to Ayalah Goren-Kadman
  for her research help at several critical junctures. I want to thank Judah Rubinstein,
  archivist, of Cleveland, Ohio, and Dr. Rafael Medoff who responded to my inquiries. I
  benefited from a close reading of an early version of this paper by William B. Goldfarb of
  Tel Aviv who shared with me his first-hand knowledge of facets of Silver's career.
1 "Zionist Memorial: Trumpeldor, 1920" (hereafter, Trumpeldor Memorial), Series V, Folder
   57, Microfilm Edition of the Papers of Abba Hillel Silver.
2 Abba Hillel Silver, *The Democratic Impulse in Jewish History*, New York, 1928, pp. 42–43.

judgment as in a leader with vision. *Such* vision is surely an apt description of Silver's celebrated role beginning about 1943 and lasting through 1948 when he was instrumental in redefining and implementing Zionism's goals. His address to the American Jewish Conference in August 1943 calling on American Jewry to close ranks in support of a Jewish commonwealth in Palestine was the opening salvo of a new strategy and a new leadership. Historians have dwelt on Silver's rapid rise to power and his astonishing success in organizing a "second front" in America to outflank the British in the struggle for the Jewish state. Overcoming Zionist opposition from within, Silver, aided by brilliant lieutenants, created a nation-wide network of Zionist cadres which launched a relentless campaign to win over American public opinion and the support of a reluctant and often inimical administration.

This discussion of Silver's "Vision of Zion" — his expectations of the *Yishuv* (the Jewish community in Palestine) in his early years, and from the *State* in his later years — focuses on his "living visions" of Zion. By that I mean neither the tactical moves of the political leader nor the learned pronouncements of the theologian. Rather, this essay considers Silver's more temporal visions which were responses — sometimes visceral ones — to developments in the *Yishuv*. To be sure, they were molded by his religious convictions and his Zionist politics, and also by his American social and political ethos. They were informed no less by a particular "Hebraic" connection to the land of Israel. Silver's ardor for the spoken language was a product of his childhood and the Hebrew cultural ambience of the home. Oft-told is the account of his precocious leadership as a teenager in the Hebrew-speaking Dr. Herzl Club. In his adult relationship with Palestine, highlighted by periodic visits to the country, being at ease in the vernacular Hebrew enabled him to establish a rapport with the *Yishuv* and gave him a sense of belonging, at least in his own mind, which played a part in his perception of the country and in shaping his expectations.

In an article Silver published in 1924, he sketched with remarkable specificity what was tantamount to his Zionist credo. Aptly entitled, "My Dream of Palestine" — which either he or the newspaper's editor subtitled, "Will the Jew Give Form to the Ideal of Palestine So Necessary for His Spirit?" — Silver expounded on the role and the nature of the Jewish National Home as he understood it. At the time, he was frequently speaking on behalf of the Keren Hayesod, the primary Zionist fund for supporting settlement work in Palestine. Prior to that, he had played a key role in the Palestine Development Corporation and headed the Central Committee of the Palestine Development League originally established by the Brandeis group for funneling private investments into specific projects in Palestine. He was thus immersed in the full gamut of the practical side of Zionist work.

In the "My Dream" article, Silver paused in the mundane task of selling shares and raising funds to consider the ultimate significance of the Zionist endeavor. In a sense the touchstone of the essay was his brief reference to the recent pogroms in the Ukraine. With the doors of America slammed shut, refugees "choking" the "highways of Europe" had focused nearly exclusive attention on Palestine as the asylum for Jews in flight. Silver took exception to this conventional plea for Palestine's importance. A place of rest and refuge for individual Jews, to be sure, he wrote, "but that is not why Israel wants Palestine. That is not why the Jewish people needs Palestine." Silver rejected a Zionism "based on pity for my unfortunate brothers." It was not the "persecuted bodies of my people that need Palestine," he asserted, as much as "the persecuted and harassed spirit of the race that needs a refuge and a sanctuary."[3]

The notion that a creative Zionist center in Palestine would reach out and strengthen Jewish cultural life in the Diaspora was of course the essence of Ahad Ha-am's teachings. For Silver, Zionism as spiritual renewal was especially attractive. In this respect he belonged to that strand of American Zionism espoused in the early years of the century by a group of rabbinical Zionists identified or close to the Jewish Theological Seminary. Israel Friedlaender and Mordecai Kaplan, of the Seminary's faculty; Judah Magnes, rabbi of the Reformed Temple Emanu-el and later the head of the New York Kehillah; and Solomon Schechter, the president of the Seminary, the illuminati of the group, offered a religious revision of the ideas of Ahad Ha-am. In the words of the historian, Ben Halpern, this religious revision of Ahad Ha-am "fitted well into the place allotted to the Jews as a religious community in the American scheme of things." In the 1920s, as was the case two decades earlier, the "harassed spirit of the race" referred to America's assimilating Jews intent upon integrating into American society with little regard for their Jewishness. In 1906 when Schechter formally affiliated with the Zionist organization, he explained that he did so because Zionism was "the mighty bulwark against the incessantly assailing forces of assimilation." In 1924, Silver declared:

> We have been able to resist organized phalanxes of hostility throughout centuries, but we have not yet learned how to resist prosperity...[and] keep our soul intact and integrant under freedom and opulence.... Our spiritual integrity seems to yield and melt away.

The only hope was

> a home for this soul of our race where it can live in a congenial environment, where it can create and evolve new and inner spiritual cultural values with which to bless mankind in the future even as it blessed mankind in the past.[4]

Precisely what were these "new and inner spiritual values?" Silver proceeded to expound on the uniqueness of the "racial soul" which had made the Jews smashers of idols, succorers of the poor, the first to preach economic and social justice, international peace, and the right of every people to live its own life. "We want Palestine because we want to give these prophetic ideals of our people a chance." Silver stood classical Reform doctrine on its head. Israel could best fulfill its mission to humanity by rebuilding the national homeland. Once more he recalled his favorite prophet: "The greatest Jew who ever preached in the most eloquent terms of the mission of Israel was the greatest Zionist, the Isaiah of the exile."[5]

Besides being inspirational, Silver's "dream" contained an *operational* dimension. Firstly, he noted that fulfilling the dream did not require millions of Jews living in Palestine. "Numbers don't count, really"; quality and devotion mattered. What was needed were "people who are caught up with this frenzy of the race." With such zealots, one could begin the cosmic venture in earnest. "I would like to see in Palestine," Silver declared, "the social, and economic, and political ideals of my people experimented with...where there will be no excess wealth, no excess poverty, but where every man really lives *tachat gafno u'tey-nato* (beneath his vine and his fig tree)." By turning Palestine into the "experimenting station of mankind, we will regain our position of leadership in the world which we have lost. That is my dream."[6]

This was the vocabulary of an American social progressive: not calling for a classless society but rather seeking a decent if not total equality. Especially interesting is the emphasis on perpetual experimentation. Only in this manner could one hope to refine and improve the social order. This was the undogmatic, open-ended, pragmatic approach of the middle-of-the road social reformer of the sort of Jane Addams, John Dewey and Louis Brandeis. Here, too, was Ahad Ha-am's cultural Zionism with its elitism, its disinterest in the political, and its emphasis on the "preparation of the hearts" for the

---

4   Ben Halpern, "The Americanization of Zionism," *American Jewish History*, vol. 69, Sept. 1974, p. 33; Solomon Schecter, *Seminary Addresses and Other Papers*, New York, 1961, p. xxiv; *The Jewish Tribune*, June 13, 1924, p. 2.

5   *The Jewish Tribune*, June 13, 1924, p. 11.

6   Ibid.

revival of the Hebraic spirit. But it was more. It was Silver's own prophetic Zionism: *malkhut shamayim* (the Kingdom of God) *in process*, Jews in the Land of Israel *becoming*, by example, "a light unto the Gentiles." It would have to be worked out; it was not preordained.[7]

In an essay published in 1929, Silver made explicit what he had implied in his "My Dream" essay. For some time past, he argued, the dominant tone of cultural Zionism had become in fact "prophetic Messianism." Its protagonists were not thinking of "just another secular culture, but of a quite unique and extraordinary culture, which, ages ago, was touched with the live coal of a prophetic inspiration." This was to be "a crusading culture" which would "transform the world, a culture of social imperatives" which would reach out "for 'new things, things kept in store, not hitherto known.'" Indeed this drive for "new things" was identical with the "ancestral hunger for *malchut shamayim*." The "historic new Jewish State" would be an expression of the historic social idealism of the race. Again, as he had more than once, Silver turned to the theme of experimentation. "Palestine must become the workshop of our people's highest aspirations and mankind's experimental laboratory for social reconstructions."[8]

Although Silver mentioned in his essay not only "the new Jewish State" but also "the renascent Jewish commonwealth," it is unlikely that at the time the terms carried the political weight they later assumed. In fact, the essay concluded with the conviction that the political phase of Jewish messianism was drawing to a close. The building of the National Home was proceeding apace. The increase in immigration and the number of settlements, the *Yishuv's* intense cultural life, and the Hebrew University on Mount Scopus, all provided proof of that progress. On the occasion of the opening of the University in 1925, he rhapsodized:

> The doors of the Third Temple are opening wide. The Schechinah returns to her home. In a hundred alien lands she wandered, an exiled Spirit, wistful, hated and abashed. She now returns in queenly grace to her own courts, and mounts her alabaster throne.

Most promising of all, the long sought-for partnership between non-Zionist Jewish wealth and the Zionist Organization — the enlarged Jewish Agency

---

7   For an account of Silver's social activism see Marc Lee Raphael, *Abba Hillel Silver: A Profile in American Judaism*, New York, 1989, pp. 36–41, 59–62. For an expression of his liberal philosophy see "The Creed of a Liberal," Series V, Folder 173, 1928, Silver microfilm edition.

8   Abba Hillel Silver, "Herzl and Jewish Messianism: Nationalism as a Means to a Greater Goal," in *Theodor Herzl, A Memorial*, edited by Meyer W. Weisgal, New York, 1929, p. 256.

— was about to be consummated, heralding a golden age of economic expansion, population growth and Jewish unity. Noteworthy in Silver's statement are the Brandeisian ideas that went back to 1920 when Silver enlisted in the Brandeis camp. With the British mandate and its recognition of the Jewish National Home ratified by international law, Brandeis had argued, Zionism no longer needed to stress political nationalism. The political infrastructure was in place; needed now was a rational, business-like policy to create the ideal social democracy. This optimism was soon to be dispelled. In August, 1929, Arab riots in Palestine produced a British policy hostile to the National Home, and the American stock market crash all but disabled the Jewish Agency. But at the time Silver wrote his essay, probably at the end of 1928 or the beginning of 1929, he believed the Zionist movement had just about achieved its political goals. The Jews were on the threshold of a transnational era. Nationalism, he declared, was certainly not mankind's ultimate vision; nor was it "the substance of our own ancestral tradition" whose motif was not "nationalism but prophetism." Silver envisioned Israel pushing "on to the frontiers of the new world — the world of internationalism, of economic freedom, of brotherhood and of peace. It must resume the burden of its Messianic career."[9]

The passage is striking and has caught the attention of scholars because it so succinctly sums up Silver's weaving of the various strands of the practical, spiritual, and political into an appealing holistic Zionism. Significantly, sixteen years later, on December 29, 1947, at a testimonial dinner in his honor, prior to his departure for Palestine to attend a crucial meeting of the Jewish Agency executive, Silver quoted the same passage in its entirety.[10] Comparing the historical context of the two occasions in which he used the same text is illuminating. In 1929, it appeared that Israel had reached its *menukha* and its *nakhala* — its tranquility and its inheritance — only to be thwarted by a shocking turn of events. The 1947 address was delivered exactly one month after the UN General Assembly had adopted the partition plan. The nations of the world had given their sanction to the establishment of a State. (When published in a volume of Silver's addresses in 1949, it was entitled, "The Month of Exaltation.") But in December 1947, the *Yishuv* was in a state of mobilization. Skirmishes, soon to become outright battles, had begun, and total war was imminent. American Jewry was uninformed of the extent of the peril the *Yishuv* faced. In the weeks ahead,

---

9 *New Palestine*, March 27, 1925, p. 335; Autobiography, G/1-8, Abba Hillel Papers, The Temple, Cleveland, Ohio.

10 Allon Gal quotes this passage when he places Silver among the exponents of the "mission motif" in American Zionism. See Allon Gal, "The Mission Motif in American Zionism (1898–1948)," *American Jewish History*, vol. 75, no. 4, June 1986, p. 382.

Silver would play a crucial role in informing American Jewry of these facts and in leading it in support of the *Yishuv's* battle for statehood. But when he spoke in December, the euphoria of the UN decision had not dissipated (although Silver pointed to the dangers that lay ahead). It was the high point of his political career, and he used the opportunity to look ahead beyond the political struggle.[11]

The soon-to-be-established Jewish state, Silver declared, promised to reach beyond narrow national concerns. The promise was evident "in the humble and consecrated labors of the present-day nation-builders in Palestine." Using terminology that had not changed over the years he drew an image of Israel, its national life secure, pushing on to the frontiers of a new world. He included in his 1947 address a rather striking sentence from his 1929 speech: "Our national rebirth was made possible by a war [World War I] in which nationalism was thoroughly exposed and discredited." (His older and more radical colleague among the Zionist Reform rabbis, Judah Magnes, would put it more provocatively: the Balfour Declaration and the Mandate were born in sin, the sin of British imperialism.)[12]

Silver, an enthusiastic supporter of the war, had been thoroughly disillusioned by the peace treaty of 1919. In several sermons that year he attacked the leaders of the victorious powers for their vindictiveness, their unabashed imperialism and their brutal flouting of the declared war aims. Little remained of Wilson's principles of self-determination and his program for a comity of nations. A year later, Silver reported on his trip to Europe. He was more hopeful. The signs of recovery from the war's devastation were everywhere to be seen; noticeable, too, was an undercurrent of a spirit of liberalism. Nevertheless, chauvinistic leaders still ruled. Silver warned, America "must not become a partner to a scheme of partitioning Europe; we must not join a band of unscrupulous imperialists in perpetuating themselves and in saddling themselves upon the back of Europe."[13]

---

11 *New York Times*, Dec. 30, 1947, p. 7.

12 *Vision and Victory: A Collection of Addresses by Dr. Abba Hillel Silver, 1942–1948*, New York, 1949, p. 153; Arthur A. Goren, *Dissenter in Zion, From the Writings of Judah L. Magnes*, Cambridge, 1982, pp. 27–28, 183–190.

13 Abba Hillel Silver, "Is the Treaty of Peace a 'Peace' Treaty," June 1, 1919, Series IV, roll 146, folder 52, Silver microfilm edition; "The Sins of the Allies," Nov. 2, 1919, idem, folder 55; "On Europe Revisited — Impressions of 1920," Oct. 10, 1920, idem, folder 80. In a sermon delivered on October 29, 1939, Silver reviewed his stand during World War I and his utter disillusionment following the peace treaty. On his attitude to the "new World War," Silver wrote: "It is a necessary war.... There is but one way of stopping him [Hitler], and that is war. But it is an evil, an unspeakable evil. And knowing my experience of the last twenty-five years, I cannot put my hope into this war, much as I would like to. I do not see it through apocalyptic eyes." Abba Hillel Silver, *Therefore Choose Life: Selection Sermons, Addresses, and Writings*, edited by Herbert Weiner, Cleveland, 1967, p. 402.

If momentarily Zionism had benefited from the intrigue of the peace negotiations, with the inclusion of the Balfour Declaration in the terms of the mandate over Palestine and its award to Britain, that fortuitous development did not invalidate Silver's long view of the imperialistic, self-interest of the great powers and most directly, Britain's policy in Palestine. Applying his strictures of 1929 to 1947, he expressed the political limitations and dangers of the international game of nationalism, a game he had observed from close range in the political struggle for the Jewish State. He knew the intrigues and the brutal power-moves as they unfolded within his own movement and on the international scene. Standing before the admiring audience that came to pay homage for his leadership in directing the battle for partition, Silver used the opportunity to press the immediate needs of the *Yishuv*. He called on the United States to supply arms to the Jewish militia of the new state. But he also rose above the politics of the hour. Even at that moment he reminded his listeners that the struggle for a state was not the ultimate goal and warned against the dangers of chauvinism. His political sensibility no less than his religious belief led him to declare once more: "Nationalism is not enough. It is a minimum requirement, not a maximum program." The present struggle for a Jewish state must end in something more than another state.[14]

That "something more," the qualitative rather than the quantitive character of the state, would be achieved, Silver had stated years earlier, by the bearers of the dream, those who come to Palestine "caught up by this frenzy of the race." It is in connection with this notion of a vanguard totally committed to the redemption of the ancestral land that an illuminating document — handwritten notes Silver prepared for a lecture on Joseph Trumpeldor — provides some remarkable insights into his understanding of the human dimension of the dream. By the time Silver composed these notes, sometime at the end of 1929 or the beginning of 1930, Trumpeldor had become a national legend of Zionist heroism and self-sacrifice. A former captain in the Russian Army who had lost an arm in the battle of Port Arthur during the Russo-Japanese War, he had immigrated to Palestine in 1912 to join a workers' commune in the Galilee. In 1915, exiled to Egypt by the Turks, he organized the Zion Mule Corps which was attached to the British Army that fought in the ill-fated Gallipoli campaign. Following the war, Trumpeldor travelled to Russia and established Hechalutz — the organization of socialist-Zionist pioneers — whose members played the dominant role in the kibbutz movement and in the Histadrut. In March 1920, he fell while commanding the defense of Tel Hai (in the Upper Galilee

---

14 Silver, *Vision and Victory*, p. 153; *New York Times*, Dec. 30, 1947, p. 7.

less than a mile from present-day Kiryat Shmoneh) against Arab marauders.[15]

The choice of the subject is remarkable in itself. The Trumpeldor myth was popular in Europe and Palestine especially among Zionist youth, but it was hardly known or used by American Zionists. No less striking was the choice Silver made in his interpretation of the Trumpeldor legend. By the late 1920s, the Trumpeldor myth had been embraced by opposing Zionist ideologies. Soon after his death, the most radical elements of the *halutz aliyah* established a country-wide communal body called *Gdud avoda al shem Yosef Trumpeldor* (Joseph Trumpeldor Labor Corps), a tribute to the founder of the *halutz* movement and the exemplar of its values. Five years later, the youth arm of the Revisionist movement — the movement that crystallized around the leadership of Vladimir Jabotinsky, the militant Zionist nationalist — named itself *Betar*, the Hebrew acronym for *Brith Trumpeldor* (Trumpeldor Alliance). The emphasis Silver gave to the story provides us with a key to *his* understanding of the process of national redemption.[16]

Movingly, Silver chronicled Trumpeldor's life and death. Jotting down fragments of sentences, he wrote:

> Trumpeldor at gate wounded: orders them [the other defenders] to rally on...wounded again...replace intestines into abdomen "I will show you" — lull — relief [Trumpeldor's last words] "It is good to die for one's country." Moved to Kfar Giladi in stretcher — died on way — buried in dead of night — 4 men and 2 girls killed — 5 wounded.

This was a "simple story," Silver continued,

> drama, heroes, grandeur which lends grandeur to Palestine.... Jews have always demonstrated physical courage...especially in fighting in defense of Palestine. Not the first — from Joshua to Bar Kokhba. The legions of Antiochus, of Titus, of Hadrian, knew how gallantly Jews fought against overwhelming odds. Trumpeldor and his comrades continued this glorious Jewish tradition.

But, Silver declared, physical heroism was not the most important lesson to draw from the Trumpeldor story. The story was significant because of his life more than his death. "He symbolizes a movement, the noblest in the 20th century, known as *halutziut*."[17]

---

15 For a brief account of Trumpeldor and the Tel Hai episode and lengthier analysis of the creation of a national myth of Jewish heroism, see Yael Zerubavel, *Recovered Roots, Collective Memory and the Making of Israeli National Tradition*, Chicago, 1995, pp. 39–47, 138–44, 147–157.

16 Ibid.

17 Trumpeldor Memorial. All quotations in the following paragraphs are from this source.

The power and nobility of the movement was the longing "for national redemption through self-redemption." Here was "great idealism — no sentimentalism...vision coupled with a cold realism and discipline." Lapsing into the first person plural — "we" — Silver disclosed the depth of his empathy for the *halutzim*.

> We can save ourselves only through work, productive, creative, honest work. And Palestine can be built up only in this manner, too. We have been luftmenschen, small fry capitalists, hangers on of an exploitive capitalist system.... Work alone will save us. We wish to be builders! on farms, on roads, in towns in graineries, in mills — anywhere, just so we build, produce, create. We will become the pioneers of a working Palestine. A new land needs our balm, a new life needs our life-force.... And we will work socially.... A new social order, less cruel, less harsh than the one we knew in the old world. The social vision of our prophets.

Silver summed up: "Our future in Palestine lies in the values of *halutziut*, not politics." Significantly, in an aside, Silver felt compelled to castigate the superficiality of American Zionism. After portraying the unbounded dedication of the *halutzim*, he wrote: "See how different this is from our Zionism. We are proxy Zionists. Our 'Judenschmerz' evaporates in expressing itself best in campaigns, at worst in talk."[18]

Silver's sentiments on *aliyah* and *halutziut* hardly went beyond the occasional expression of admiration for the *halutzim* in Palestine who were in the vanguard of creating his vision of Zion. However, beginning in 1945 *halutziut* and *aliyah* from America was placed on the Zionist agenda, albeit with much reluctance, primarily by the insistence of the *Yishuv's* heads. Leaders in Hadassah and the ZOA distanced themselves from the debate. It is in this light that Silver's comments before a meeting of the American Zionist Emergency Council held in December 1945 assumes their significance. Reporting to the council on his return from a meeting of the Jewish Agency executive in Jerusalem, he described the warm welcome he had received in these words:

> The *Yishuv* felt that there was today a complete concordance between the kind of Zionism we represent here and the kind of Zionism they represent there.... They were particularly interested in one thing, and that is in American Chalutziut.

18 Ibid.

Silver then related how he had informed his Jerusalem colleagues that a cable from America contained the information that one thousand American *halutzim* had completed their *hakhshara* work and an additional six hundred were waiting for certificates to immigrate. Silver continued: "They [the *Yishuv's* leaders] want to tap this great reservoir of five million American Jews for the upbuilding of Palestine.... That will be the next great task that will confront American Zionism." Silver expounded on the benefits American *halutzim* would bring to the process of "nation building." They would act as a leavening force, forge another link between Palestine and the United States, and introduce "some of the American ideas into the country."[19]

Silver's belief in the *halutz* ethos, the creation and core ideal of the socialist-Zionist movement, did not preclude his inclination to embrace a Zionist geography that approached if it was not identical with the Revisionist program. He came to this position, it appears, immediately upon the rise of Hitler to power. In the spring of 1933, Silver spent a month in Palestine during his sabbatical year abroad. It was an exhilarating visit. During the six years since his previous visit, the *Yishuv* had made enormous strides. Coming from Germany, the contrast was awesome as it was distressing. Silver had been present in Berlin when the Nazis took power, and he had witnessed gangs of Nazi hoodlums whipping up the crowds into a frenzy of anti-Semitism. Silver was convinced that Germany's Jews must evacuate the country, and the *Yishuv* made ready to receive them. He expressed these sentiments in a talk he gave in Tel Aviv. Silver addressed the audience in Hebrew. (His handwritten text of the speech is written in flawless, idiomatic Hebrew.) Perhaps because of the audience, the place, the language, his closing words were especially grandiloquent.

> And now it is clear to all of us. We need a spacious haven, no mere corner, nor a narrow, fenced-in place, as Eretz Yisrael is today, divided into two. Rather, from the desert and the Lebanon unto the great river, the Euphrates, all the land of the Hittites to the great sea, will be our boundary. And to this haven our brothers will come.... In this place, on both sides of the Jordan (*al shtey gadot ha-Yarden*) we will create our new life.

The boundaries were those promised to Abraham by God, and the phrase, "*shtey gadot la-yarden*," was the motif of the Revisionist Zionist hymn. Significantly, during his month in Palestine, Silver toured Transjordan with Nelson Glueck as his guide. He jotted down this brief note at the start of the

---

19 American Zionist Emergency Council, Minutes of Meeting Held December 24, 1945, Central Zionist Archives.

tour: "Greater Palestine — more fertile — under separate mandate — should be opened for Jewish colonization." *Shtey gadot la-yarden* was no mere rhetorical flourish.[20]

Out of such an emotional linkage — the divine promise of a redeemed Israel secure in its idyllic boundaries, spoken in the Hebrew tongue in the Hebrew city of Tel Aviv, then beheld from the heights of Moab, and the unfolding disaster he had witnessed in Germany — flowed a geographic vision that Silver found hard to compromise with. In 1935, at the convention of the Zionist Organization of America, he demanded that the delegation about to leave for the forthcoming World Zionist Congress be instructed to urge that the opening of Transjordan to Jewish immigration be made "the spear point" of political effort to resolve the Palestine problem. "It must now become part of the land of promise for the millions of our people who have to go there."[21]

His vehement opposition to the decision of the Jewish Agency executive in the summer of 1946 to secretly propose partition to the Americans and the English stemmed not only from his view that a horrendous diplomatic blunder had been made. It flowed at least in part from an emotional tie to the physical Land. When the time came to compromise — to support partition and to accept a "truncated" state — "the man of vision and cold realism" did so. He even infused it with a higher meaning. "The Land of Israel will be small, made smaller by partition, but the people of Israel will make it great. The monumental contributions to civilization have been made by great peoples which inhabited little countries. Mind and creative endeavor will compensate for what our people have been forced reluctantly to relinquish."[22] Just as nationalism should be transcended once a people was rooted in their soil so the constrictions of space could be transcended in matters of the spirit.

Silver entered the tumultuous period of the final push to statehood and the no less tumultuous period that followed guided by the same articles of faith — political, spiritual, cultural — he had maintained from the beginning of his public career. Assuring the security of the new-born Israel was the first order of the day, and Silver devoted all his energies to the task so long as he was permitted to do so. From May 15, 1948, such matters became the exclusive domain of the State. For a time Silver fought doggedly to assure the World Zionist Organization and its most powerful segment, the American movement, a public role as a formal partner in the process of state-building.

20 A Hebrew Address in Tel Aviv, 1933, Series V, Folder 318, Silver microfilm edition.
21 Annual Report of Zionist Organization of America, 38th Annual Convention, Atlantic City, June 30–July 2, 1935, p. 221.
22 Silver, *Vision and Victory*, p. 154.

But it was of no avail, and by early 1949 over the specific issue of control of the fund-raising apparatus, Silver was forced to retire from active leadership.[23] In a more discreet manner he maintained his interest in the unfolding domestic scene in Israel. In this sphere he brought the convictions of a tried and true American liberal.

As a political activist in American life he had supported labor and progressive social legislation, and he had insisted upon the social responsibilities of the well-off in contributing to the common good. These convictions, he believed, also fit the *Yishuv's* and then the state's political scene. They also formed, he assumed, the basis for a good rapport with the labor movement. For years, he had lent a hand to the Histadrut's fund-raising campaigns in America and praised labor's achievements. During his 1945 trip to Palestine, which coincided with the 25th anniversary of the founding of the Histadrut, he addressed the jubilee convention in Hebrew acclaiming the pioneering role of the Histadrut and its social experimentation which he saw as a striving for *tikkun olam* (repair of the world). However, as an American progressive, Silver emphasized the primacy of individual freedom, the opportunity it offered through free choice for economic and social growth, and he expressed his distrust for dogmatic ideologies. In a brief statement which he formulated in 1929 — a manifesto-like declaration, "The Creed of a Liberal" — he enunciated "the primacy of [the individual's] claims over the claims of all forms of human organization." This was the highest principle of civil behavior. He believed in a freedom that was "compatible with the fullest measure of responsibility." The only "tools of social progress" he emphasized, "are education, experimentation and cooperation." Consequently, "the very motive power of progress" required "the free exchange of ideas and the exercised privilege of nonconformity."[24]

In American politics, Silver is best defined as an independent progressive Republican. In many respects, the social policies he favored were identical with Franklin D. Roosevelt's New Deal program. This sort of elasticity, acceptable in American political life, was beyond comprehension in the political culture of Israel. Whether Silver ever intended to take part in Israeli political life either as the recognized head of a powerful American Zionist movement, which is likely, or by actually settling in Israel, as some hoped, is less important than the fact that this American liberal was out-of-joint with Israeli politics. For Labor his social reform was not rigorous enough nor anchored in socialist doctrine. Moreover, the collectivist, disciplined "party"

---

23 Raphael, *Silver*, pp. 174–202.
24 Series V, roll 173, file 173, Silver microfilm edition. In addition to the typescript, the file contains three printed clippings dated March and November 1929 and an undated clipping from the *Louisville Unitarian*.

— the "partei," *ha-miflaga* — was wary of the individualist and outsider. And insofar as temperament and broad policy are concerned, Silver felt more comfortable with the General Zionist party in Israel, the "sister movement" of the Zionist Organization of America, which indeed honored and adulated him. But the factionalism and partisanship organic to Israeli politics (including the General Zionist camp) in due time dampened whatever ardor Silver may have had to participate directly or indirectly in the political life of Israel.[25]

In one important respect, Silver found enormous personal satisfaction during these years — and the fulfillment of an important part of his Zionist vision. His ability and success during his visits to the land of Israel during the pre- and post-state period to communicate with the Israeli masses in their own vernacular drew upon the Hebraic core of his Zionism. An incident at the start of his public career illuminates this component of Silver's Zionist creed. In 1917 when his Zionist integrity was questioned by none other than Stephen S. Wise for accepting the pulpit of a classically Reform temple at the price, rumor had it, of compromising his Zionist activity, Silver expressed his Hebraic-Zionism in these succinct words. He had come to Zionism, he told Wise, "through my love of Hebrew Culture and Literature and for the mighty promises which it holds as a 'galvanizing force' in Jewish life."[26] This Hebraic core of his Zionism remained a constant. Few American Zionist leaders possessed his facility with the Hebrew language or his devotion to its cultivation. In one respect his "Hebraism" came to fruition in his unmediated meetings with the Israeli masses. Several instances of his public addresses to the *Yishuv* underscore his success in stirring his Israeli listeners and in turn being profoundly moved by the experience.

In December 1945, within hours of his arrival in Palestine to attend a meeting of the Actions Committee of the World Zionist Organization, his first visit in eight years and a time of political uncertainty and tension in the country, he spoke to the *Yishuv* over the government-controlled radio during

---

25 For a detailed treatment of this period and Silver's connection with Israeli politics, see Noach Orion, "The Leadership of Abba Hillel Silver on the American Jewish Scene 1938–1949," (Hebrew), PhD dissertation, Tel Aviv University, 1982; Melvin Urofsky, *We Are One: American Jewry and Israel*, New York, 1978, pp. 279–318; Raphael, *Abba Hillel Silver*, pp. 73–182, 197–205. Writing to Emanuel Neuman from Jerusalem summing up his first visit following the end of World War II (which he judged as "all positive"), Silver described the internal politicization of the *Yishuv*. The fact that he came as President of the ZOA, defined him as part of the General Zionist camp and in part explained the cool reception he received. See Orion, pp. 272.

26 Quoted in Michael A. Meyer, "Abba Hillel Silver as Zionist Within the Camp of Reform Judaism," paper delivered at Brandeis University Conference on Abba Hillel Silver. See p. 15 in this volume.

the scheduled Hebrew transmission. Efforts by government officials to censor the broadcast failed. Silver brought greetings from American Jewry and the assurance of its total support, and he expressed his admiration for the *Yishuv*'s accomplishments and its determination to achieve statehood. The independent daily, *Ha-aretz*, was full of praise for the content and the delivery. (The news report complimented Silver on his pronunciation which "had only the minutist trace of 'Amerikaniut.'") *Davar*, the Histadrut daily, admired the "qualities of Jewish rootedness" that distinguished him from the other leaders of American Jewry.[27]

On his next visit in March 1947, Silver was feted by being made an honorary citizen of Ramat Gan, a municipality near Tel Aviv which was dominated by the General Zionist party, a fact which gave the ceremony political overtones. His address was nevertheless nonpartisan. He spoke to all Israel. The news reports in the General Zionist daily *Ha-boker* carried the banner line: "Silver on His Two Citizenships, Eretz Israel and the U.S.: 'The founding fathers of America drew upon the wells our forefathers sunk in this Land.'" Before a packed auditorium Silver, speaking in a "superb Hebrew," explained that he had been a citizen of this "lovely land" since his childhood. However, "politically, I am a citizen of the United States."[28] The two went hand in hand. Silver ranged across the spiritual similarities between America and Israel, the democratic principles that both shared and the pioneering tradition so important to each society. Describing his impressions of the courage that he found everywhere as a united *Yishuv* faced the military rule imposed by the British, Silver concluded with the belief that soon "many Jews will come from the United States to settle in the Land, to become citizens, and may it be given to me that one day I, too, will come to build my home here amongst you." *Ha-aretz* ran the story under the headline: "Many Jews from the United States will come to settle in Eretz Israel." These were the words the embattled *Yishuv* wanted to hear.

Once again, in the spring of 1951 after more than a two-year absence, Silver returned to the country to receive an enthusiastic but manifestly partisan reception. (The confrontations between Silver and Ben-Gurion over their opposing views on Diaspora Zionism, power-sharing with the Jewish State, and external support for Israeli political parties — the Knesset elections were approaching — are beyond the scope of this essay although they obviously cast a giant shadow over Silver's visit.) Made an honorary citizen of Tel Aviv, cheered by thousands as his motorcade passed through the city's streets, and addressing an overflow audience of 30,000 at a public

27 *Ha-aretz*, Dec. 9, 1945 (or 47), p. 2; see also Yishiyahu Veinberg, *Abba Hillel Silver: Life, Vision, Achievement* (Hebrew), Tel Aviv, 1957, p. 125; *Davar*, Dec. 12, 1945, p. 2.
28 *Ha-boker*, March 27, 1947, p. 4.

meeting, Silver once again proved himself to be the great communicator. He called for the unity of the Jewish people and expounded on the new tasks a revitalized Zionism must shoulder in assuring the well-being of Israel. Twice more on that visit he addressed the nation through the state radio. Eventually, the political acrimony between Silver and Ben-Gurion abated. In his later visits in the 1950s and 1960s, he spoke of his visions of an unfolding Israel to all sectors of the nation.[29]

In June 1915, Silver, the twenty-two year old valedictorian of his Hebrew Union College class, entitled his address: "Dreams and Visions." In 1952, he returned to the College to deliver the commencement address. On this occasion he chose the title, "There is Yet Room for Vision." He recalled the verse from the prophet Joel that had inspired the title of his valedictorian address: "Your old men shall dream dreams, your young men shall see visions." As a newly ordained rabbi he had expounded on the text: "Age dreams of the days that were. Youth has visions of the days to come." His peroration was an ode to Reform where the dream of the past had not been allowed to crush the vision of the people. The commencement address was no less an ode to Reform Judaism but woven into its fabric were the Zionist ideals he had also expounded from the pulpit in the intervening years. Having so recently played the major role in the political struggle for the Jewish state, Silver sought to place the momentous event in a religious-historical context. The *galut* — exile — had indeed come to an end. Israel was now prepared to receive all those for whom Diaspora life was intolerable or unsatisfying. There remained, however, the messianic vision of the establishment of the good society of universal justice, a vision of the *aharit ha-yamim*, that reached far beyond national restoration and the achievement of sovereignty. Once more he stated, as he had from his early years in the pulpit, that this Messianic vision would unfold first in the land where it was initially enunciated, Israel. Silver's visions were inspired by three equally powerful stimuli: a profound religiosity, a Hebraic-Zionism that evoked an intimacy for the land of Israel, and the Realpolitik of Jewish need. In concert they distinguished his Jewish nationalism.[30]

29 *Ha-Aretz*, April 25, 1951, p. 1; April 26, pp. 2, 8; April 29, p. 2; April 30, p. 4; Vinograd, *Silver*, pp. 258, 260, 269–270, 298. *New Palestine*, May 1951, vol. 41, no. 9, p. 2. See also Raphael's discussion in *Silver*, pp. 175–202, 204–215. Raphael discusses briefly the invitation made to Silver in 1952 to accept the presidency of the Hebrew University. Silver made his acceptance contingent upon Ben-Gurion supporting the proposal. Ben-Gurion refused to support or oppose the invitation.

30 Silver, *Therefore Choose Life*, pp. 13, 15, 434–35, 441.

Where American Zionism Differed:
Abba Hillel Silver Reconsidered

Mark A. Raider

IN 1917 ABBA HILLEL SILVER, the rising twenty-four year-old star of the Reform movement, was offered the pulpit of The Temple-Tifereth in Cleveland, Ohio. The Temple's selection committee was especially concerned about Silver's Zionist views and scrutinized him thoroughly. In the end, the committee was satisfied by Silver's assertion that Zionism aimed to "galvanize Jewish life the world over" and that, in any event, a Jewish state would neither erase the diaspora nor "be detrimental to the status of the Jews in America."[1]

When Stephen S. Wise, the prominent Reform rabbi and distinguished Zionist leader, learned of Silver's appointment and negotiations with The Temple, he interpreted his junior colleague's pronouncement as an effort to appease the local layleaders. "I believe that it may be true," Wise wrote to Silver in May 1917, "that you would not have been called to the pulpit of the congregation if it were felt that you were a warm and unequivocal supporter of the Zionist movement and ideal." Wise urged Silver to search his "conscience" and to "correct this impression at the earliest possible moment."[2]

Wise's letter evoked a sharp response from Silver who insisted that he welcomed all expressions of Jewish nationalism "as so many dikes against the onrushing tides of assimilation." Moreover, Silver declared, he considered himself "a disciple of Ahad Haam."[3]

> And any suggestion which would intimate that I have revised or modified my views in order to "pass muster" for my new post in Cleveland is downright calumny and slander. The pulpit of Tifereth Israel was graciously *offered* to me. There have been absolutely no conditions or tacit agreements involved in the matter. I go to Cleveland a free and independent man — and I am convinced that my people there would not be content with any other.[4]

1 Quoted in Marc Lee Raphael, *Abba Hillel Silver: A Profile in American Judaism*, New York/London, 1989, p. 28.
2 Stephen S. Wise to Abba Hillel Silver, May 7, 1917. P-134/119, Stephen S. Wise Papers, American Jewish Historical Society (hereafter Wise Papers).
3 Abba Hillel Silver to Stephen S. Wise, May 11, 1917, Wise Papers.
4 Ibid., emphasis in original.

This early episode prefigures the trajectory of Silver's career as a Zionist leader. In the beginning, Silver, an East European immigrant, was an "outsider" in the Reform movement and his credentials were, to a large degree, suspect. Likewise, Silver's Zionist allies feared the young rabbi's professional ambitions might prompt him to jettison his Zionist commitments. In both respects, however, Silver proved to be an unrepentant iconoclast. He neither assented to his congregation's classical Reform outlook, nor did he hesitate to denounce what he considered to be a distortion of his philosophical perspective. He stood, he insisted, foursquare within the camps of Reform Judaism and Zionism.

The case of Abba Hillel Silver also reflects the turbulent decades that spanned World Wars I and II. His meteoric rise and fall raises important and interesting questions about the nature of American Zionism and American Zionist leadership. Silver rose to national prominence at a moment in history when the Jewish people faced questions about its very survival. At a pivotal moment he used his authority to galvanize public opinion and shape American Jewish policy vis-à-vis the Jewish National Home and postwar reconstruction. He may not necessarily have been more important than other American Zionist leaders, but his stewardship was, arguably, more crucial than that of Louis D. Brandeis, Stephen S. Wise, Louis Lipsky, Henrietta Szold and others. Silver's unique style of leadership did not derive from his standing among the American Jewish elite. Nor did it issue from profound philosophical expositions or his position as rabbi of one of America's largest Reform congregations. Even his oratorical prowess does not fully explain his grasp on American Jewry. Where Silver's Zionist leadership differed was his talent for independent political action.

I. Silver's Zionism in His Early Years

Born in Lithuania on January 28, 1893, Abraham Silver (as he was originally known) immigrated to the United States at the age of nine. Growing up on New York's Lower East Side, young Abraham was immersed in the fluid setting of the Jewish immigrant milieu. He saw no contradiction between attending public school, yeshiva and Zvi Hirsch Masliansky's sermons at the Educational Alliance. In 1904, following the death of Theodor Herzl, he co-founded the Dr. Herzl Zion Club.

After graduating high school, Silver enrolled in Hebrew Union College and the University of Cincinnati. On several occasions, he arranged for prominent Zionists to speak at the then predominantly anti-Zionist Hebrew Union College. In this period he also changed his name to Abba Hillel. He graduated from both institutions in 1915 and was ordained a rabbi.

Following a brief appointment in Wheeling, West Virginia, Silver

WHERE AMERICAN ZIONISM DIFFERED

assumed the prestigious pulpit of The Temple-Tifereth in Cleveland, Ohio. As noted, The Temple's lay leaders were apparently undaunted by Silver's Zionist views. They were more interested in his oratorical abilities and growing reputation. Silver did not disappoint his congregants, and during his tenure The Temple's membership skyrocketed. Meanwhile, he became something of a local icon. He was the first president of the local Bureau of Jewish Education, chairman of Cleveland's Jewish Welfare Fund Appeal, a leader in the campaign for unemployment insurance and, until he resigned in protest over the treatment of local labor unions, a member of the Chamber of Commerce.[5]

During the 1920s, at the urging of Stephen S. Wise and other prominent members of the so-called "Brandeis group," Silver intensified his involvement in American Zionist affairs. In 1921, however, as a result of the conflict between Louis D. Brandeis and Chaim Weizmann over the future of the Zionist Organization, he officially resigned along with the Brandeis group from the leadership of the Zionist Organization of America (ZOA). He nonetheless continued to participate in national Zionist activities.[6] He was especially active in efforts to enlarge the scope of the Palestine Development Council (PDC). Founded in 1921, the PDC supported a wide range of projects in Palestine. Silver also played an important role in establishing the group's satellite Palestine Development Leagues (PDL) in the United States.[7] The purpose of the PDL was to aid in the

> social economic upbuilding of Palestine so that it may be populated within a comparatively short time by a preponderating body of manly, self-supporting Jews endowed with the highest Jewish ideals and fitted to become citizens of a self-governing commonwealth.[8]

The PDC and the PDL enjoyed the staunch backing of Louis D. Brandeis, Felix Frankfurter, Julian W. Mack, Stephen S. Wise and other members of the Brandeis group. The latter used the PDC as one of several avenues for circumventing the policies of the new ZOA administration headed by Louis Lipsky. Lipsky himself was supported by Chaim Weizmann, Brandeis' chief rival.[9] Despite competition from the Zionist Organization's Keren Hayesod

---

5 Marc Lee Raphael, *Abba Hillel Silver*, chs. 1–2.
6 See Melvin I. Urofsky, *American Zionism From Herzl to the Holocaust*, Garden City, 1975, ch. 7.
7 "Palestine Development Council." A/405-XII-42a, Julian W. Mack Papers, Central Zionist Archives (hereafter CZA).
8 Directory of National Organizations, *American Jewish Year Book*, Vol. 23, 1921, p. 247.
9 Jehuda Reinharz, *Chaim Weizmann: the Making of a Statesman*, New York/Oxford, 1993, p. 342.

[Palestine Foundation Fund], the PDC's propaganda campaign was a marked success. In fact, it attracted the participation of many non-Zionists and former anti-Zionists.[10]

Silver made persistent efforts to promote the Zionist cause among his Reform colleagues. Though officially anti-Zionist prior to 1937, the Central Conference of American Rabbis (CCAR) had previously expressed "a willingness to work for the economic upbuilding of Palestine." The PDL, Silver proposed, "affords [the CCAR] a chance for such service."[11] Silver initially wrote to Dr. Edward N. Calisch, president of the CCAR, in the hope of circulating a letter that would endorse the PDL's objectives. Calisch, however, insisted upon reorganization the PDC board as a prerequisite for his assistance. Consequently, Silver reverted to his original plan of "win[ning] the cooperation of the men in the ministry for the work of the Leagues in their various communities."[12]

While Silver served as chairman of the PDL central committee, he rapidly became enmeshed in the politics of fundraising that permeated Zionism and American Jewish life. The experience strengthened his conviction that American Zionism's future hinged on a combination of broad popular support and close collaboration with the World Zionist Organization (WZO). This stance contrasted with that of the Brandeis group and, from the latter's perspective, came perilously close to the attitude of the ZOA's Lipsky-led faction. As a result, Silver found himself increasingly at odds with other members of the Brandeis group. At a November 1922 meeting, Louis D. Brandeis and Felix Frankfurter berated Silver for his heretical views. The event precipitated Silver's resignation from the PDL and the PDC. Although he blamed his resignation on increasing professional demands, he also explained to Julian W. Mack that

> the program of [Louis D. Brandeis] for the raising of funds... is doomed to utter failure, and with it, I fear will come the ultimate dissolution of the PDC.... We have been unable to interest the few rich people, and I fear that shall be unable to interest them in the future. *Not that we have not tried but that we have tried and failed....* Our hope lies with the many fairly well-to-do; and in order to reach these larger numbers, an effective organization of paid workers

10 Stephen S. Wise to Abba Hillel Silver, January 9, 1922, Wise Papers.
11 Abba Hillel Silver to Stephen S. Wise, October 13, 1921, Wise Papers.
12 Stephen S. Wise to Abba Hillel Silver, October 10, 1921; Abba Hillel Silver to Stephen S. Wise, October 13, 1921; Stephen S. Wise to Abba Hillel Silver, October 15, 1921; Abba Hillel Silver to Stephen S. Wise, October 24, 1921; Stephen S. Wise to Abba Hillel Silver, November 7; Stephen S. Wise to Abba Hillel Silver, November 11, 1921; Stephen S. Wise to Abba Hillel Silver, November 18, 1921; Stephen S. Wise to Abba Hillel Silver, December 26, 1921, Wise Papers.

and organizers as a basis for volunteer work is the sine qua non. I have urged this for eighteen months. I have failed to convince the organization.[13]

Additionally, Silver noted that he felt "the attacks of LDB and FF [on him] were particularly unjust and ungracious." He warned that he would not tolerate further "judicial admonitions" and "professorial casuistry."[14]

Silver's resignation from the PDC and the PDL did not deter him from finding ways to assert his influence as a Zionist activist. Throughout the 1920s he sustained a busy schedule of national lectures on behalf of the Zionist cause. In 1924 — the year that his parents immigrated to Palestine — Silver openly supported the Keren Hayesod campaign and emerged as one of its most vocal proponents.[15] In 1929 he was elected a delegate to the Sixteenth World Zionist Congress and a vice president of the Zionist Organization. The Zionist Congress was held in Zurich from July 28–August 10, 1929, and heralded the enlargement of the Jewish Agency for Palestine by including non-Zionists. The Labor movement in Palestine began its rise to power and Yosef Sprinzak, Shlomo Kaplansky and Arthur Ruppin, spokesmen for the *Yishuv* (the Jewish community in Palestine), joined the Zionist Executive.

Silver welcomed these developments as constructive steps in the solidification of the Zionist enterprise. His experience in national and international Zionist affairs affirmed his faith in a variegated approach to building the Jewish National Home.[16] Though he identified most fully with the ZOA's General Zionist platform, his favorable disposition toward the Zionist pioneers associated with the Labor movement dated back to 1919 when he first toured the *Yishuv*. Upon his return to the United States, Silver glorified the hard working *halutzim* [pioneers] of the rural colonies and agricultural settlements.[17]

Silver's memorial address for the Zionist hero Joseph Trumpeldor, who was killed in March 1920 during a battle for the defense of a Jewish outpost in Upper Galilee, exemplifies his adulatory perspective. Unlike the Zionist leader Vladimir Jabotinsky, for example, who coopted Trumpeldor's image to symbolize a right-wing agenda later embodied by the Revisionist Zionist

13   Abba Hillel Silver to Julian W. Mack, December 4, 1922, Wise Papers, emphasis in original.
14   Ibid.
15   See, e.g., the following speeches by Abba Hillel Silver on the Keren Hayesod: February 4, 1925 and April 27, 1925 (reel 172); 1926 (reel 173). Microfilm Edition of Abba Hillel Silver Papers, Brandeis University Libraries (hereafter Silver Papers).
16   See, e.g., the following speeches by Abba Hillel Silver on Zionism: "Palestine protest meeting, 1929" and "Louis Marshall memorial, 1929," Reel 174, Silver Papers.
17   "Palestine as I Saw It," October 12, 1919, Reel 146, Silver Papers.

youth movement Brit Trumpeldor [Covenant of Trumpeldor, Betar], Silver venerated the socialist Zionist idealism of the fallen leader.[18] "Our future," Silver declared, "lies in [the] realm of *halutziut* [pioneering] — not politics." He claimed that the story of Tel Hai demonstrated that Jewish "national redemption" could only be achieved through "self-redemption." He called for the creation of new pioneering settlements and declared that the social vision of *halutziut* was the fulfillment of biblical prophecy in the modern age.[19]

Silver's attitude toward the Labor enterprise was the product, in large measure, of two confluent streams of thought. On the one hand, the messianic proclivity of the immigrant milieu and Silver's own East European upbringing implanted in him an openness and sensitivity to the utopian aspirations of the *halutzim*. On the other, having grown to maturity in the United States, Silver also imbibed a strong "Ahad-Haamist" sensibility that was well suited to Jewish idealism in the American context.[20] Above all, the core of Silver's Zionism was an unswerving devotion to Judaism. "The prophetic element in Zionism," he asserted, "is not the exuberant dream of a few romanticists."[21]

> It is present in the thought of its most sober and realistic exponents... Hitherto wanting the full complement of the attributes of nationalism, we were constrained to overemphasize its virtues. Many of the spokesmen of our cause were driven to extol nationalism *per se*, which is after all a quite recent, and demonstrably, a quite inadequate human concept. It is not mankind's ultimate vision. Certainly it is not the substance of our own ancestral tradition, whose motif is not nationalism but prophetism. Nationalism is not enough. It is a minimum requirement, not a maximum program.... After its national life is secure Israel must push on to the frontiers of the new world — the world of internationalism, of economic freedom, of brotherhood and of peace.[22]

Silver continued to promote what he perceived to be Zionism's vital role in rejuvenating modern Jewish life and uplifting humanity. "Zionism, as I see it," he explained to Avukah [The Torchbearer] college Zionists in 1932,

---

18 See Gideon Shimoni, *The Zionist Ideology*, Hanover/London, 1995, pp. 232–235; Mark A. Raider, *From the Margins to the Mainstream: Labor Zionism and American Jews, 1919–45*, Ph.D. diss., Brandeis University, 1996, ch. 3.

19 "Zionist Memorial, Trumpeldor," 1920, Reel 171, Silver Papers.

20 See Evyatar Friesel, "Ahad Haamism in American Zionist Thought," in *At the Crossroads: Essays on Ahad Haam*, ed. Jacques Kornberg, Albany, 1983, pp. 133–141.

21 Abba Hillel Silver, "Herzl and Jewish Messianism: Nationalism as a Means to a Greater Goal" in *Theodor Herzl: A Memorial*, ed. Meyer W. Weisgal, New York, 1929, p. 256.

22 Ibid.

aims at the classic balance in Jewish life. Judaism is a compound of many elements. Many tributaries flow into its historic channel — prophecy, legalism, mysticism, nationalism. In recent years some zealous and mostly uninformed partisans have attempted to reduce Judaism to what is only a fraction of itself — to race or nationalism or folk-ways or theologic abstractions. Quite unconsciously they are falsifying Judaism. It is a mark of our decadence in the diaspora that so many of our people have lost the sense of the classic harmony in Jewish life and are attempting to substitute a part for the whole. Zionism is the national effort to restore the lost harmony of Jewish life. It aims at a reconstituted totality of Jewish existence.[23]

II. Silver's Pragmatism

With the rise of Adolf Hitler to power, Silver was one of the first American Jewish leaders to speak out against the threat of Nazi aggression and anti-Semitism. As early as 1933, in opposition to many prominent American Jews, he advocated a boycott of German-made goods and co-founded the League for Human Rights Against Nazism, an enterprise that foreshadowed his involvement in the Non-Sectarian Anti-Nazi League to Champion Human Rights.

Silver's vigorous support of the boycott did not, however, preclude his subsequent qualified support of the Haavarah [Transfer] Agreement. The Trust and Transfer Office Haavarah Ltd. was created through the initiative of Labor Zionist leader Chaim Arlosoroff following an agreement with the Nazi regime in August 1933. The agreement made possible the emigration of Jews to Palestine by allowing the transfer of their capital in the form of German export goods. Between 1933 and 1939, the Haavarah facilitated the emigration of approximately 60,000 German Jews to Palestine and the transfer of more than forty million dollars which was used for the immigrants' social and economic absorption.[24]

In the United States and elsewhere, the Haavarah was criticized for weakening the boycott of Germany. Abba Hillel Silver, like Stephen S. Wise, initially decried the scheme. "The very idea of Palestinian Jewry

---

23 Abba Hillel Silver, "The Total Program," in *The Brandeis Avukah Annual of 1932: A Collection of Essays on Contemporary Zionist Thought Dedicated to Justice Louis D. Brandeis*, ed. Joseph Shalom Shubow, New York, 1932, p. 42.

24 Leni Yahil, *The Holocaust: The Fate of European Jewry*, New York\Oxford, 1990, pp. 100–104; *Encyclopaedia Judaica*, vol. 7 (1972), pp. 1012–1013.

negotiating with Hitler about business," he exclaimed, "instead of demanding justice for the persecuted Jews of Germany is unthinkable."[25] Despite his rhetoric, Silver's paramount concern remained alleviating the plight of German Jewry. After the Nineteenth Zionist Congress approved strict guidelines for the Haavarah in 1935, Silver gave his conditional support to the plan. Later, in instances when the Zionist regulations appeared to have been breached, Silver's position was clear and forthright. For example, in November 1935 the *Palcor News Letter* carried a statement by a representative of the citrus growers in Palestine that arrangements had been made whereby some 400,000 cases of Palestine oranges would be exchanged for German goods. This statement, Silver, exclaimed "is startling inasmuch as it is a clear violation of one of the internal resolutions of the Lucerne Congress..."[26]

> ...The important thing is to know whether the Zionist Executive now in complete charge of the Transfer, is following up faithfully the terms of the agreement arrived at the Lucerne Congress, namely: 1. The Transfer is to be used only for those Jews who are actually emigrating to Palestine. 2. No German goods are to be sold through the Haavarah in the Near East outside of Palestine. 3. The Haavarah is not to be used for the purpose of barter arrangements between the orange growers of Palestine and the Nazi government.
>
> If the Executive of the Agency is living up to these agreements, there is nothing further that we can do about the matter. If it is not, then we must demand a compliance with the agreements or a total scrapping of the Haavarah.[27]

Silver's pragmatic approach to Zionist and Jewish affairs was also clear in the early 1930s when he went head to head with the ZOA's local leadership. Eventually, he withdrew from the Cleveland Zionist District and formed Cleveland Zionist District No. 2. The new group, renamed the Cleveland Zionist Society, rapidly outgrew its counterpart. Subsequently, the ZOA leadership negotiated a settlement that brought Silver's group and their dues into the national organization.[28] In another instance, *The Temple Bulletin* published excerpts from the avowedly secular Labor Zionist journal *Jewish Frontier* on topics such as "Hitler and Nietzsche" and "The Prayer of German Jewry."[29] Melbourne Harris, Silver's assistant rabbi from 1935 to 1944, edited

---

25 *Jewish Daily Bulletin*, August 30, 1933.

26 Abba Hillel Silver to Stephen S. Wise, November 20, 1935, Wise Papers.

27 Ibid.

28 Marc Lee Raphael, *Abba Hillel Silver*, ch. 3.

29 See e.g., *The Temple Bulletin*, vol. XXII, no. 10, December 29, 1935, pp. 3–4, Wise Papers.

the bulletin. It is certain, however, that the bulletin would not have reprinted these items without the senior rabbi's tacit approval.

While Silver himself was never a proponent of the left, he did maintain a respectful attitude toward American and Jewish labor. He was a staunch defender of union interests in Cleveland, because of moral and ethical considerations, not partisan inclinations.[30] He defended the rights of American Jewish Communists, even when such support was not politically advantageous. Such was the case in 1937 when Silver publicly refuted the accusations of Rev. Dr. E. Freking, spokesman for the Catholic Students' Mission Crusade, who criticized the Central Conference of American Rabbis for its declaration of sympathy with the Loyalist Government in Spain. In contrast to Rabbi Morris S. Lazaron, who denounced "secularism among Jews" and asserted that "no believing Jew can be a Communist,"[31] Silver unapologetically noted that it was "not unfriendliness to the Catholic Church nor sympathy with Communism that prompted [the Reform] resolution."[32] However, he asserted,

> ...If there are some Jews in the United States who are Communists, there are also Communists among the German, Irish, Italian and other nationality groups in this country. If some Communists come from Jewish homes, others come from Catholic and Protestant homes. And, be it remembered, there are as vigorous opponents of Communism among Jewish leaders in this country as there are among Catholic or Protestant leaders. These leaders, in the name of democracy, oppose Fascism as vigorously as they do Communism which, unfortunately is not always the case with Catholic leaders.[33]

The foregoing statement depicts, at least implicitly, Silver's faith in the potentiality of the left. His belief in the need to improve the social and economic conditions of the toiling and the disenfranchised classes resonated with the mission ethos of Reform Judaism.[34] It also made possible his ongoing relationship with groups like the League for Labor Palestine and the National Committee for Labor Palestine. While Silver never wholeheartedly

---

30 Marc Lee Raphael, *Abba Hillel Silver*, pp. 35–41.
31 Morris S. Lazaron, "Jews and Communism," *American Hebrew*, July 2, 1937, p. 4.
32 Abba Hillel Silver, "Are American Jews Communists?" *American Hebrew*, July 2, 1937, p. 4.
33 Ibid.
34 See Abba Hillel Silver, "Israel" in *Year Book of the Central Conference of American Rabbis*, ed. Isaac E. Marcuson, vol. 45 (Central Conference of American Rabbis, 1935), pp. 327–328; Allon Gal, "Universal Mission and Jewish Survivalism in American Zionist Ideology," *From Ancient to Modern Judaism, Intellect in Quest of Understanding: Essays in Honor of Marvin Fox*, eds. Jacob Neusner, et al., vol. 4, Atlanta, 1989.

endorsed the Labor Zionist program — e.g., he was not an avid proponent of the 1935 Reform declaration in favor the Histadrut[35] — he did sustain warm relations with these groups. He appeared at Labor Zionist conferences, participated in the movement's national events and conventions, and maintained open relations with Rabbis Samuel Wohl, Felix Levy, James Heller, Barnett Brickner and Edward L. Israel, all of whom were active in Labor Zionist affairs, as well as Joseph Schlossberg of the League for Labor Palestine, Isaac Hamlin of the Jewish National Workers' Alliance, Baruch Zuckerman of the Poalei Zion party and Hayim Greenberg, editor of *Jewish Frontier*.[36] Silver was also responsive to American Hechalutz, a Labor Zionist group that trained young men and women for kibbutz life in Palestine.[37]

Silver did not support and was less tolerant of Revisionist Zionism which during the 1930s became embroiled in a protracted struggle between Vladimir Jabotinsky, the movement's founder, and the Palestinian leader Abba Achimeir who rejected democracy and embraced the model of Italian fascism.[38] Silver also generally distrusted the separatist tendencies of the Zionist right-wing.[39] Silver's perspective is explained, in part, by the fact that he categorically opposed "all Fascist, Nazi and Communist governments and movements." He declared, "I believe them to be a menace to civilization. I am opposed to them regardless of whether under those regimes Jews are persecuted or not."[40] Consequently, when Vladimir Jabotinsky visited the United States in 1926 and wrote that he felt "unwelcome in Cleveland," Silver did nothing to alter Jabotinsky's perception.[41] Moreover, in the 1930s and 40s when Revisionist Zionists sought to establish a foothold in the United States, Silver actively maintained his distance from the Zionist right.[42]

---

35 Mark A. Raider, *From the Margins to the Mainstream*, pp. 95–97.
36 See, e.g., Abba Hillel Silver, "Speech to Dinner Meeting of the League for Labor Palestine," November 21, 1933, Reel 47; Samuel Wohl to Abba Hillel Silver, September 28, 1934, Reel 47; Telegram of Felix Levy, James Heller and Barnett Brickner to Abba Hillel Silver, January 28, 1936, Reel 47; Abba Hillel Silver to Edward L. Israel, January 28, 1936, Reel 47; Isaac Hamlin to Abba Hillel Silver, March 27, 1944, Reel 31; Joseph Schlossberg to Abba Hillel Silver, November 3, 1944, Reel 31, Silver Papers.
37 Nathan Guttman to Abba Hillel Silver, June 6, 1938, Reel 64, Silver Papers.
38 Joseph Heller, *The Stern Gang: Ideology, Politics and Terror, 1940–1949*, London, 1995, p. 4
39 See Yaacov Shavit, *Jabotinsky and the Revisionist Movement, 1925–1948*, London, 1988, ch. 2.
40 Abba Hillel Silver to John M. Powers, April 13, 1938, Reel 2, Silver Papers.
41 Vladimir Jabotinsky to Abba Hillel Silver, March 23, 1926, Reel 33, Silver Papers.
42 Joseph B. Schechtman, *Rebel and Statesman: The Vladimir Jabotinsky Story, The Early Years*, New York, 1958, pp. 388–394; Chanoch (Howard) Rosenblum, "The New Zionist Organization's American Campaign, 1936–1939," *Studies in Zionism*, vol. 12, no. 2, Autumn 1991, pp. 169–185; Elias Ginsburg, "Is Revision-Zionism Fascist? [sic]" *Menorah Journal*, vol. 22, no. 2, October–December 1934, pp. 190–206.

Silver's position vis-à-vis Jabotinsky, which was more than a tactical maneuver, is particularly revealing when compared to that of other Zionist leaders. Indeed, he allowed Stephen S. Wise and Hayim Greenberg, editor of *Jewish Frontier*, to set the terms of the public debate over Revisionism. Wise decried Jabotinsky's "unmistakably Fascist sympathies and his anti-Labor Party conduct."[43] Greenberg persistently attacked Revisionism as a "sinister movement of frank Fascist hooliganism."[44] Meanwhile, it was left to the philosopher Horace M. Kallen to seize the moral high road. What was really at stake, Kallen insisted, was the fundamental principle of liberty of speech and expression. He wrote:

> ...I am opposed to Jabotinsky in terms of his basic program, but I am also opposed to denying the leader of an opposition party and the spokesman of a view contrary to mine a hearing... I am therefore making a gesture, not for Jabotinsky's platform and program, but his right under a democratic conception of human relations to present his principle and program for serious consideration of all people...[45]

As these responses illustrate, the climate of American Jewish opinion was generally antipathetic to the Revisionist cause.[46] Moreover, while the leadership of the Jewish Agency, the *Yishuv* and American Zionism sought to marginalize Revisionist Zionism, Silver himself remained conspicuously silent.[47] It is particularly striking that Jabotinsky, a Zionist leader of international stature, was rebuffed by Wise and Greenberg (two of the diaspora's premier Zionist spokespersons), defended by Kallen (a Labor Zionist proponent) and ignored by Silver (a Zionist centrist). Given Silver's remarkable success in such endeavors as the Palestine Development Council in the 1920s, the Nazi boycott of the 1930s and, at a later stage, enterprises such as the United Palestine Appeal and the American Zionist Emergency Council, it is telling that he did not lend even tacit support to Revisionist

---

43 Stephen S. Wise to Horace M. Kallen, February, 21, 1940, 317/16:243, Horace M. Kallen Papers, YIVO Institute for Jewish Research (hereafter Kallen Papers).

44 Hayim Greenberg, "Revisionism: A Self-Portrait," *Jewish Frontier*, vol. 2, no. 3, January 1935, p. 15. Other examples of Greenberg's writings are: "Jabotinsky's Army Marches," *Jewish Frontier*, vol. 2, no. 3, January 1935, p. 6; "The Threat of Revisionist Irresponsibility," *Jewish Frontier*, vol. 5, no. 8, August 1938, pp. 7–9; "The Irresponsible Revisionists," *Jewish Frontier*, vol. 10, no. 11, November 1943, pp. 6–8.

45 Horace M. Kallen to Stephen S. Wise, February 23, 1940, Kallen Papers.

46 Chanoch (Howard) Rosenblum, "The New Zionist Organization's American Campaign," pp. 169–185.

47 Pierre M. Atlas, "Defining the Fringe: Two Examples of the Marginalization of Revisionist Zionism in the 1930s," *Israel Studies Bulletin*, vol. 9, no. 2, Spring 1994, pp. 7–11.

Zionist efforts. In the final analysis, Jabotinsky's efforts to generate political and monetary support in the United States were totally unsuccessful.[48]

Silver's political pragmatism and non-dogmatic Zionism, exemplified by his stand on a variety of issues in the 1930s, anticipated much of his later Zionist activity and leadership on a national level. In an era when most Jewish and Zionist leaders placed a premium on the notions of "belonging" and "deference," Silver shunned partisan loyalties. He held very definite views, but he was not doctrinaire. His approach to Jewish life embraced a range of liberal and conservative positions. That Silver himself recognized the underlying strength of such pluralism, both as a spiritual and political leader, was evident from the start.

III. Years of Crisis: 1937 to 1939

The Fortieth Annual Convention of the ZOA served as the backdrop for Silver's reentry to the arena of national Zionist politics. The convention was held in July 1937, just days before the British Royal Peel Commission released its official findings. It was generally assumed that the commission's report would result in the cantonization or partition of Palestine into Arab and Jewish entities. At the time of the Peel investigation, no American Jewish consensus existed concerning the political future of the Yishuv.[49] However, by 1937 a significant number of Jewish communal organizations and leaders had gone on record in favor of building the Jewish National Home.[50]

Silver was one of a handful of American Zionist leaders who, like the Yishuv leaders, grew increasingly wary of Chaim Weizmann's gradualism and distrusted Great Britain. Fearful that the British government intended to limit the size and growth of the Jewish National Home, Silver made a passionate appeal to the ZOA convention's largely pro-Weizmann constituency.[51] He argued that a Jewish polity in a partitioned Palestine was neither viable nor a solution to the Jewish problem. Silver correctly anticipated the Peel Commission's partition proposal and used the opportunity to clarify his understanding of Zionism's historic, religious and political dimensions.

---

48   Chanoch (Howard) Rosenblum, "The New Zionist Organization's American Campaign," p. 169.

49   See "Opinion in American Jewish Daily Press is Divided," *Jewish Frontier*, vol. 4, no. 8, August 1937, p. 30.

50   See Mark A. Raider, *From the Margins to the Mainstream*, ch. 6.

51   The ZOA's continued support for Chaim Weizmann is noted in "Review of the Year 5699 — United States," *American Jewish Year Book*, vol. 41, 1939, p. 231.

To the problem of Palestine today there is no other logical solution than that which the Zionists have been advocating ever since 1917 — a complete and loyal fulfillment of terms of the Mandate.... We had a right to ask that — not only on the basis of the [Balfour] Declaration and the Mandate and the international approval which was given to both, but on the basis of the concrete achievement of the Jews within Palestine during the last twenty years.... Certain arrangements with reference to Palestine may be forced upon us. However, we shall not accept them. We shall continue to work, to advocate, to educate until such time as the just claims of our people are established. We have no right to sign away the historic claims of the Jewish people nor the future of our children. We have no right to pledge future generations to a political arrangement which is in consonance neither with the hopes, the history nor the religious convictions of our people.[52]

When in July 1937 the Peel Commission recommended that Palestine be partitioned into separate Arab and Jewish states, the response of American Jews to the commission's proposal was mixed.[53] A minority of American Zionists adhered to a set of maximalist demands and refused to renounce Jewish claims to any part of Mandatory Palestine including Transjordan. Meanwhile, Jewish Communists, Bundists, supporters of Brit Shalom and renegade members of the American Jewish Committee and the Jewish Labor Committee coalesced around the call for a binational solution to the Arab-Jewish conflict in Palestine. Finally, the Zionist mainstream — a broad coalition of General Zionists, Labor Zionists and unaffiliates — were reluctant to publicly oppose Britain.[54] They adopted the Jewish Agency's initial strategy of non-rejection of the partition proposal with the understanding that outright rejection of the plan might eventually be necessary to protect Zionist interests.[55] This approach reflected the twin influences of Palestine's dominant Mapai party and American Zionist pragmatism.[56] Such a strategy was well attuned to the interests of American Zionism's old guard. The Brandeis group, explained Julian W. Mack, "is unalterably opposed to partition."[57]

---

52 "ZOA Convention, New York City," June 28, 1937, Reel 178, Silver Papers.
53 *Palestine Royal Commission Report, July 1937*, London, 1937, p. 394.
54 Marc Lee Raphael asserts that the "large majority of the American delegation [to the World Zionist Congress], despite Silver's oratory, favored the [partition] plan." See Marc Lee Raphael, *Abba Hillel Silver*, p. 74.
55 See Robert Szold's address to the Hadassah Convention of October 1937, A406/168, Robert Szold Papers, CZA [hereafter Szold Papers]; "The Hadassah Resolution on Partition" (editorial), *The Reconstructionist*, vol. 3, no. 14, November 19, 1937, pp. 3–4.
56 Itzhak Galnoor, *The Partition of Palestine: Decision Crossroads in the Zionist Movement*, Albany, 1995, pp. 75–76.
57 Julian W. Mack to Emanuel Mohl, October 5, 1937, Szold Papers.

If ultimately it should be imposed upon us, then, of course, we want to have the best and largest possible State, but so far as we are concerned, it will be an imposed and not an accepted State... In our judgment the situation is continuously changing, and decisions as to tactics taken at one time are necessarily subject to change at other times and under other conditions.[58]

General opposition to the Peel proposal brought Silver back into the fold of the Brandeis group.[59] Like those at the helm of the *Yishuv* and the Zionist Organization, however, he also recognized the urgent need for mass immigration to Palestine and large-scale colonization.[60] As a result, although he publicly denigrated the partition proposal, privately and *sub rosa* he strove to prepare for the possibility of its realization under optimal conditions. This activist stance, shared by a minority of Zionist leaders in the United States and the leadership of the *Yishuv*, portended an important realignment in world Zionist politics.[61]

The new situation thrust Silver, whose ramified Zionist outlook was hitherto suspect by American Zionism's old guard, back into the political limelight. In August 1937 Silver was a delegate to the Twentieth Zionist Congress in Zurich which considered the Peel Commission's proposal. He strenuously opposed the commission's recommendation to "separate the areas [of Palestine] in which the Jews have acquired land and settled from those which are wholly or mainly occupied by Arabs." In the end, however, he submitted to the position of "non-rejection" endorsed by a majority of the Congress which called on the Zionist Executive to negotiate a modified proposal with the British.[62]

Despite Silver's strained relations with the American Zionist establishment, he was assiduously courted by Stephen S. Wise and others. The reason for this was, in part, that Silver possessed extraordinary organizational skills and unique oratorical talents. He also demonstrated a flare for harnessing the financial and political energies of American Jewry.[63]

---

58 Ibid.

59 Stephen S. Wise to Abba Hillel Silver, May 28, 1937, Reel 64, Silver Papers.

60 See the statement of the American Economic Committee for Palestine written by Robert Szold, Congressional Record — Appendix, August 3, 1937, pp. 10505–10507.

61 Stephen S. Wise to Abba Hillel Silver, December 20, 1937, Reel 64, Silver Papers.

62 *Palestine Royal Commission Report, July 1937*, p. 382; *Palestine Post*, August 12, 1937, pp. 1, 4; *Palestine Post*, August 15, 1937, p. 1; *Palestine Post*, August 16, 1937, pp. 1, 4; *American Hebrew*, August 13, 1937, pp. 7, 15; *American Hebrew*, August 20, 1937, pp. 1, 6, 15; *American Hebrew*, August 27, 1937, pp. 1–3, 10, 12, 17, 22.

63 Melvin I. Urofsky, "Rifts in the Movement: Zionist Fissures, 1942–1945," *Herzl Year Book* (1978), vol. 8, pp. 200–201.

In fact, when Silver accepted the chairmanship of the UPA in 1938, so confident was Wise in his junior colleague that he exclaimed:

> It is for younger men like yourself to begin to assume the responsibility which we older men have carried too long. I am not asking to be relieved of responsibility. I am perfectly willing act as coadjutor to you and to be Chairman of the Executive Committee here, assuming that you wish it. Be perfectly frank and tell me if you think it would be better for me not to be Chairman so as to make clear that a new regime has come. I will understand.[64]

No sooner had Silver assumed the head of the UPA than he set about consolidating his own base of support within the Zionist movement. He aligned himself with competent and efficient young men such as Henry Montor, Emanuel Neumann and Harold Manson who, like Silver, adhered to an assertive General Zionist philosophy and independent political stance. He also conducted UPA policy without consulting the ZOA leadership and, in effect, directed a sphere of political activity independent of the American movement as a whole. In this way, Silver began cultivating an inner circle of his own — a group that would later be known as the "Silverites."

As UPA chairman, Silver was determined to bring the American Zionist movement into close collaboration with the WZO and the Labor-led *Yishuv*. In his first address as national chairman of the UPA he outlined "the amazing story of Jewish pioneering work and achievement in Palestine."[65]

> During the past year, in spite of the unsettled political conditions in Palestine, nineteen new settlements were founded... A new port was built in Tel Aviv... With the investment of substantial public funds, such as the United Palestine Appeal is endeavoring to raise in the United States, the economic activities of Palestine will be greatly stimulated and increased opportunities will be created for a much larger immigration... The World Budget which was set up by the Jewish Agency for Palestine, composed of Zionists and non-Zionists alike, calls for seven and three-quarters millions of dollars.... It is my profoundest hope that American Jewry, in its traditional generosity, will rise to the challenge of this grave hour and make possible the upbuilding of the land.[66]

One year later all Zionist hopes were dashed when Britain retracted the partition scheme and declared it impracticable. In May 1939 London issued

---

64 Stephen S. Wise to Abba Hillel Silver, January 6, 1938, Wise Papers.
65 "United Palestine Appeal, 1938," Reel 179, Silver Papers.
66 Ibid.

the MacDonald White Paper which placed a cap on the growth of the
Yishuv and closed the doors of Palestine to Jews in distress. The new British
policy shocked and enraged American Zionists. Silver, who during the
intervening period had also become co-chairman of the United Jewish
Appeal (UJA), joined other ZOA leaders in calling an emergency
conference in Washington, D.C. At the conference he reiterated the need
for constructive Zionist work on all fronts, particularly the realization of
Britain's commitment to the establishment of an autonomous Jewish
National Home.[67] In an unusual move, the conference censured anti-
partition and maximalist Zionist groups who refused to honor the decision of
the recent Zurich congress. With Silver's strong support, the ZOA
administrative committee passed an unprecedented resolution barring all
"unauthorized" Zionist political activity that undermined the Jewish
Agency's negotiations with the Mandatory Power. It was hoped that such a
policy would strengthen American Jewish forces who recognized the need for
united political action.[68] In this instance, as in others, Silver's UPA policies
were congruent with the interests of the Labor-led Yishuv.

Silver also strove to reign in and, when possible, resolve the contentious
rivalries between different Zionist groups. In this way, he sought to
consolidate the Palestine fundraising energies of American Jewry. He began
by insisting on a strict accounting of monies raised on behalf of the Jewish
National Home. For example, he opposed the use of UPA funds to
underwrite the building of the popular Palestine Pavilion at the 1939 World's
Fair. "The UPA was not established to raise money for pavilions, to advertise
for Palestine," he wrote to the eminent jurist Jonah Goldstein in 1938, "but
for colonization work in Palestine."[69] He also instructed the UPA's executive
director Henry Montor to pressure the tenaciously independent Poalei Zion
and Mizrahi parties to desist from separate fundraising campaigns that
interfered with the overall work of the UPA. The Labor Zionist
Geverkshaftn campaign, Montor reminded Isaac Hamlin, is supposed to
endeavor "to obtain money from labor sources which cannot ordinarily be
reached by such an institution as the [UPA]."[70] In another instance, Montor
criticized "the disservice being rendered to the [UPA] by the Mizrahi
Organization."[71]

67 Morris Fine, "Review of the Year 5699," *American Jewish Year Book* (1939), vol. 41, p. 200.
68 Ibid.; "Revisionism Redivivus," *Reconstructionist*, vol. 5, no. 15, November 24, 1939, p. 5;
    "Correspondence," *Reconstructionist*, vol. 5, no. 16, December 8, 1939, pp. 13–16.
69 Abba Hillel Silver to Jonah J. Goldstein, July 28, 1938, Wise Papers. Silver eventually
    agreed to a loan of $150,000 to build the Palestine Pavilion. Abba Hillel Silver to Stephen
    S. Wise, May 26, 1939, Wise Papers.
70 Henry Montor to Isaac Hamlin, February 25, 1938, Reel 64, Silver Papers.
71 Henry Montor to Leon Gellman, May 27, 1939, Reel 64, Silver Papers.

I appreciate how you and others in Mizrahi may feel with regard to the necessity of raising additional money for your Mizrahi publication in Palestine [*Hazofeh*, The Scout], but unless we can truthfully say to all contributors that they are fulfilling their obligations to Mizrahi when they give to the [UPA], we prejudice our right to include the Mizrahi and injure the [UPA]... It is not the amount involved but the principle which is at stake.[72]

In the arena of general Jewish fundraising, Silver was an equally staunch defender of mainstream Zionist interests. He was even willing to risk communal unity to ensure that Zionist projects not be jeopardized. The litmus test in this regard proved to be the battle over control of the United Jewish Appeal. In the late 1930s, the dispute, which hinged on competition for funds between the Zionist UPA and the non-Zionist Joint Distribution Committee (JDC), grew into a public controversy that generated considerable inter- and intra-organizational strife.[73] Silver, who played a key role in the conflict, conducted a cautious but aggressive policy vis-à-vis the JDC. "Unless seriously provoked," he wrote to Stephen S. Wise early on, "we ought not to engage in any controversy... Our position is not as strong as it might be. At such a time, discretion is the better part of valor."[74] A series of negotiations between the two camps — eventually joined by all the major American Jewish organizations — revealed the deep philosophical chasm that separated Zionists and non-Zionists on the eve of World War II. Zionists, Silver explained to JDC chairman Paul Baerwald, were "profoundly interested... in the refugee problem," but believed that it could "not be properly treated without reference to Palestine."[75] Meanwhile, the non-Zionist camp insisted that the distribution of funds for overseas relief should not be contingent on the needs of the *Yishuv*.[76]

The dispute was not fully resolved until late in 1941 when, after intense communal pressure, the UPA and the JDC reached an agreement that facilitated the UJA campaign of 1942. By this time, however, the national uproar over the plight of European Jewry, compounded by the unwillingness of the Allied nations to accept Jewish refugees, dictated an arrangement that substantially benefited the Zionist position.[77] Time had vindicated Silver's assertion that American Jewry would recognize "the necessity of assisting

72 Ibid.
73 Menahem Kaufman, *An Ambiguous Partnership: Non-Zionists and Zionists in America, 1939–1948*, Jerusalem/Detroit, 1991, ch. 1.
74 Abba Hillel Silver to Stephen S. Wise, December 20, 1937, Reel 64, Silver Papers.
75 Abba Hillel Silver to Paul Baerwald, November 15, 1938, Wise Papers.
76 Yehuda Bauer, *My Brother's Keeper: A History of the American Jewish Joint Distribution Committee, 1929–1939*, Philadelphia, 1974, pp. 166–168.
77 Menahem Kaufman, *An Ambiguous Partnership*, pp. 62–70.

thousands of Jews into Palestine and maintaining all those [Zionist] projects and institutions which have already been established."[78] In the spring of 1939, for example, in opposition to the American Jewish Congress headed by Stephen S. Wise, Silver withheld his support of a refugee proposal put forward by George Rublee, the American director of the Intergovernmental Committee on Refugees. The Rublee plan would have resulted in funneling a half million dollars from the UJA to a non-Zionist agency responsible for the emigration of German Jewish refugees and the transfer of Jewish capital to new host nations. "I would strongly advise against it," Silver wrote to Wise. "Certainly we ought to do nothing without authorization from the Executive of the Jewish Agency in Palestine."[79]

> What would be involved is the taking of one hundred fifty thousand to two hundred thousand dollars of money that would go to Palestine directly, to finance a project which only indirectly may benefit Palestine... It seems to me that at this time, when Palestine is clamoring for more and more funds, and when efforts are being made and will have to be made by us to raise additional funds outside of those raised in the united national campaign, we ought not to vote away Palestinian funds for any projects outside of Palestine however worthy they may be.[80]

A few months later, when the need for transporting immigrant refugees to Palestine and relief of the *Yishuv* became especially dire, Silver again deferred to the Labor-led Zionist Executive. His perspective on the distribution of American Jewish resources revealed an internal tension concerning the movement's priorities. He clearly felt, however, that nothing should be done which could jeopardize the stability of the *Yishuv*. "Should we, at this moment, concentrate on sending all the available money into Palestine so as to avert a major collapse," he exclaimed,

> or should we use part of our funds to transport additional immigrants into the country who, by the way, might still further increase the relief burden of the Yishuv? Frankly, I am unable to answer this question. It seems to me that we should depend in large measure upon the judgment of our Executive... There is, of course, terrific pressure brought to bear from our distressed refugees in all parts of Europe. But is not our first responsibility to look after the minimum needs of those already in the country, and our institutions there?[81]

---

78 Abba Hillel Silver to Stephen S. Wise, December 20, 1937, Reel 64, Silver Papers.
79 Abba Hillel Silver to Stephen S. Wise, May 26, 1939, Wise Papers.
80 Ibid.
81 Abba Hillel Silver to Stephen S. Wise, October 19, 1939, Wise Papers.

Though Silver's political strategy became increasingly aligned with that of the *Yishuv* leadership during World War II, he did not reach a public rapprochement with the key figures in the Zionist Executive — David Ben-Gurion, Berl Katznelson, Moshe Shertok (later Sharett) and others — until Hitler's forces overran Poland in September 1939.[82] Prior to this time, Silver's lukewarm relations with the Mapai leaders were due largely to his reluctance to withdraw his public support of Chaim Weizmann as well as his own sense of political independence. Nor did Ben-Gurion's low estimation of Silver help matters.[83] As late as August 1939, in sharp contrast to the emerging Zionist consensus, Silver opposed the program of "illegal" immigration known as Aliyah Bet. At the Twenty-first Zionist Congress, he publicly accused the Labor-led Jewish Agency and its supporters of pursuing policies that antagonized the British government and resulted in the cancellation of legal immigration. He urged the Labor leaders to "refrain from desperate acts of opposition, from civil rebellion, from non-cooperation."[84]

Silver's attack on the policies of the Zionist Organization provoked tremendous consternation. He, in turn, was castigated by Berl Katznelson in an address that electrified the Congress. Katznelson not only extolled the national virtues of "illegal" immigration to Palestine but called for broadening the program's scope of operations. The attitude of Silver and his supporters, Katznelson remarked, showed little appreciation for the *Yishuv*'s daily struggles and its unique role in Jewish national redemption:

> From this podium remarks were made yesterday by Rabbi Silver which I cannot permit myself to ignore. It was as if he cast a stone at our refugees on the high seas and stabbed Zionist policy in the back.[85]

The preponderant majority of congress delegates, including the Americans, concurred with Katznelson's point of view. In an unusual move, the American General Zionists convened a private meeting in order to assess Silver's statement and the delegation's official stance. In the end, the delegates unanimously rejected Silver's views and declared that he spoke only in his "personal capacity."[86]

---

82 Abba Hillel Silver to Israel Goldstein, July 28, 1938; Abba Hillel Silver to Stephen S. Wise, May 26, 1939; Abba Hillel Silver to Stephen S. Wise, October 19, 1939, Wise Papers.

83 Shabtai Teveth, *Ben-Gurion: The Burning Ground, 1886–1948*, Boston, 1987, p. 693.

84 *Palestine Post*, August 21, 1939, p. 1.

85 Quoted in Anita Shapira, *Berl: The Biography of a Socialist Zionist*, Cambridge, 1984, p. 278.

86 *Palestine Post*, August 21, 1939, p. 2.

The Twenty-first Zionist Congress and the subsequent invasion of Poland by Nazi Germany marked a watershed for Silver. Since the days when he originally broke with the Brandeis group, he had sided consistently, at least in public, with Chaim Weizmann's strategy of Zionist gradualism within the framework of restrictions imposed by the Mandatory.[87] Meanwhile, behind the scenes, he continued to promote practical and constructive steps for building up the Jewish National Home that were being carried out by the Labor enterprise in Palestine. In the wake of the events of August and September 1939, Silver's faith in Weizmann's leadership and cautious policies was completely shattered.

As the situation of European Jewry worsened and the *Yishuv*'s viability came into question, Silver quickly ascertained that American Zionism's wartime interests, which required massive communal support, could paradoxically result in policies harmful to the Jewish nationalist cause. The crux of the problem, as Silver saw it, was the reliance of the American Zionist establishment on the policies of Chaim Weizmann and the good will of the Roosevelt administration. "We are asked not only to withhold criticism of outrageous acts on behalf of the Palestine government," he asserted,

> but actually... to become apologists for the Palestine government and to make its position "understood among the Jews of America." In the meantime England intends to pursue her policy of appeasing the Arabs even more aggressively than she did before. We are also being asked not to embarrass the [Roosevelt] administration in Washington. In this way we practically acknowledge not only that the United States government will do nothing to help us in affairs touching Palestine; but also tie our hands and silence our voice in the name of American patriotism. This is an intolerable situation into which we are being moved. Every people speaks up for its own rights in these desperate times, and for its own needs.[88]

Silver was acutely aware of Zionism's tenuous position in American Jewish life. He recognized that most American Jews believed European Jewry and the *Yishuv* would, as during World War I, somehow survive the war. In contrast, Silver viewed the future with trepidation and uncertainty. The only way to avert massive human and political disaster for the Jewish people, he believed, was to rally American Jewry's nationalist impulse in defense of the Zionist enterprise. This meant creating a revolution in American Jewish life,

87 Marc Lee Raphael, *Abba Hillel Silver*, p. 79
88 Abba Hillel Silver to Emanuel Neumann, December 2, 1940, Wise Papers, emphasis in original.

and he aimed to start by replacing American Zionism's old guard with vigorous new leadership.[89]

IV. Wartime Leadership

The Zionist dissidents grouped around Silver first emerged as a political force during the tenure of ZOA president Solomon Goldman, a fiercely independent rabbi from Chicago. Goldman, who served from 1938 to 1940 in what was then American Zionism's top leadership position, sought unsuccessfully to strengthen his grasp on the movement's organizational machinery. Goldman's task was complicated by his personal distrust of Louis Lipsky and Lipsky's supporters, a large number of whom comprised the ZOA's local leadership, and his ambivalent attitude toward the Brandeis group. Moreover, Goldman felt undermined by Silver, with whom he maintained a long-standing rivalry that dated back to the 1920s when they were both young rabbis in Cleveland.[90] As ZOA president, Goldman frequently suspected Silver of secretive plots and attempts to sabotage his authority.[91] Stephen S. Wise, who himself began to view Silver as a rival in this period, nurtured Goldman's suspicions and wrote to him about "the unfriendliness and impossibility of doing anything with Silver."[92]

For his part, Silver did little to ease tensions with Wise, Goldman and other ZOA leaders. He antagonized Wise and his supporters by conspicuously refusing to join either the American Jewish Congress or the World Jewish Congress, neither of which, he asserted, were "an essential part of [the] Zionist ideology or program." In fact, many Zionists objected to both organizations on "practical and theoretic grounds," he argued, and "vast sections of American Jewry [were] definitely hostile" to them.[93] In other instances, such as the ongoing struggle for Zionist funds, the ZOA leadership resented Silver's autocratic and, at times, abrasive style. For example, Silver once wrote to Louis Lipsky that "New York City has too many meetings and too many speeches but not enough workers and direct personal solicitation on behalf of Palestine."[94]

There were also times when Silver circumvented the authority of ZOA leaders. This was certainly the case in the aforementioned UPA-JDC

89 Abba Hillel Silver: An Appreciation, New York, 1963, pp. 11–12.
90 Marc Lee Raphael, Abba Hillel Silver, pp. 70–72.
91 Solomon Goldman to Stephen S. Wise, January 20, 1939, Wise Papers.
92 Stephen S. Wise to Solomon Goldman, January 19, 1939, Wise Papers.
93 Abba Hillel Silver to Stephen S. Wise, June 4, 1936, Wise Papers.
94 Abba Hillel Silver to Louis Lipsky, May 11, 1938, Reel 64, Silver Papers.

negotiations which Silver conducted virtually single-handed.[95] Likewise, in June 1939 Silver sailed to London to discuss wartime Zionist policy with Chaim Weizmann and Eliezer Kaplan, the treasurer of the Jewish Agency. Silver's departure prior to the annual ZOA convention was interpreted as an effort "to avoid the pain of being present at the convention under [Goldman's] leadership and the spectacle of [Goldman's] re-election."[96] In short, many of Silver's actions and directives as UPA chairman embarrassed and irritated the ZOA leadership. Silver and his supporters viewed themselves as an independent political wing of American Zionism. Silver's pattern of unilateral behavior, combined with his imperious demeanor, exasperated Goldman. In February 1940 the embattled ZOA president confided to Wise that "my days of Zionist 'leadership' are at an end. If I could step out today without embarrassing you and few other friends, I would do so."[97]

Goldman, Wise, Lipsky and other ZOA leaders were no doubt fearful of Silver's pretensions to assume the mantle of American Zionist leadership. In fact, shortly after the Twenty-first Zionist Congress Silver's associates advocated that he become a contender for the position of ZOA president. Emanuel Neumann, a clever political strategist who was then working for the Jewish Agency, was among those who sought to engineer Silver's trajectory from the movement's periphery to its center. He "urged [Silver] to devote himself to the political problems facing the Zionist movement and to give vigorous and aggressive leadership to the Zionists of America." At this juncture, however, Silver, who was accustomed to the seemingly non-partisan role of UPA chairman, professed disinterest in becoming ZOA president. Even so, he did not dismiss the notion entirely. At the opportune moment, he responded to Neumann, "I may do what you suggest."[98]

In the meantime, the ZOA, with the backing of the resurgent Brandeis group, elected the businessman and philanthropist Edmund I. Kaufmann to succeed Solomon Goldman. The Brandeis group assumed that a Kaufmann administration would yield more readily to its directives than Goldman had done. Kaufmann, however, was neither a determined Zionist nor an effective leader, and his presidency created a leadership vacuum in the ZOA.[99] These circumstances opened up new possibilities for tactical maneuvering, notably the potential for "outsiders" and other Zionist groups to assert political control. One venue in this regard was a new agency called the Emergency Committee for Zionist Affairs.

95 Stephen S. Wise to Solomon Goldman, April 3, 1939, Wise Papers.
96 Stephen S. Wise to Solomon Goldman, June 16, 1939, Wise Papers.
97 Solomon Goldman to Stephen S. Wise, February 29, 1940, Wise Papers.
98 Quoted in Emanuel Neumann, *In the Arena*, p. 147.
99 Ibid., pp. 149–150.

The Emergency Committee was created as an inter-Zionist entity in the fall of 1939. Like the Provisional Executive Committee for General Zionist Affairs led by Louis D. Brandeis in World War I, the Emergency Committee was created by all the Zionist parties, with the sanction of the Zionist Executive, in order to safeguard Zionist interests during the war. The committee's staff included the exceptional organizational talents of Emanuel Neumann and Meyer Weisgal, but it was hampered by unavoidable competition with the ZOA, the World Jewish Congress and the Jewish Agency. The latter groups, although they professed support of the Emergency Committee, zealously guarded their distinct partisan interests.[100] This situation set the stage for Silver to enter the political fray.

On the eve of World War II, tension on the American Zionist scene was further exacerbated by the mounting political rivalry between Chaim Weizmann and David Ben-Gurion. Over the years, both figures had steadily cultivated separate spheres of Zionist and Jewish communal support in the United States. Beginning with the creation of the Keren Hayesod in 1921, Weizmann had developed close ties with many leading American Jewish figures including non-Zionists and wealthy philanthropists.[101] Ben-Gurion, on the other hand, had relatively few connections with elite American Jews. However, owing to his exile in the United States during World War I, when he helped to establish the Jewish Legion, Ben-Gurion was intimately familiar with the Zionist rank and file and the East European immigrant milieu.[102]

Ben-Gurion advocated restructuring the American Zionist movement and was deeply suspicious of Chaim Weizmann's overtures in the United States.[103] Impatient with Weizmann's general policy of Zionist moderation, he asserted that the movement's first priority in the United States was "not to try to convert the non-Zionists to Zionism, but rather to make Zionists out of the Zionists."[104] In December 1940 he traveled to the United States and undertook a whirlwind campaign to persuade the American movement to boldly support Zionist demands for a Jewish army and a Jewish state. Recognizing the special political value of American support for the Jewish National Home, Ben-Gurion agreed to modify some of his American tactics. Thus, for example, though definitive about his postwar vision of the *Yishuv*, he used the word "commonwealth" instead of "state" in public utterances. In the end, despite Ben-Gurion's strenuous propaganda efforts, he garnered

---

100 Ibid., p. 150; Melvin I. Urofsky, "Rifts in the Movement," p. 202.
101 Jehuda Reinharz, *Chaim Weizmann: The Making of a Statesman*, New York/Oxford, 1993, ch. 9; Menahem Kaufman, *An Ambiguous Partnership*, ch. 1.
102 See Shabtai Teveth, *Ben-Gurion*, chs. 7, 8 and 38.
103 See Allon Gal, *David Ben-Gurion and the American Alignment for a Jewish State*, Jerusalem, 1991; Shabtai Teveth, *Ben-Gurion*, pp. 688–689.
104 Quoted in Shabtai Teveth, *Ben-Gurion*, p. 776.

little support for his position. "I found one exception," he later reported to the Mapai Central Committee, "to the all-pervasive Jewish timidity in the United States — Rabbi Silver."[105]

While developments of the period prompted Weizmann and Ben-Gurion to perceive Silver as a potential ally, Goldman, Wise, Lipsky and others viewed him as an ascendant rival. The first real test of Silver's strength was the Biltmore Conference of 1942, an American Zionist gathering held in New York City in lieu of a wartime Zionist Congress. The three chief issues addressed by the Biltmore Conference were the political future of Palestine, the Arab problem, and the feasibility of creating an American Zionist alliance.

At Biltmore, Silver reformulated the American Zionist program anew. He urged the movement to embrace the Zionist Executive's combative approach and unite behind a common platform for Jewish statehood. In a rhetorical blow to the conference's pro-Weizmann forces, Hadassah and other groups that hesitated to support forceful Zionist action, he decried the "unreal, spurious and dangerous" distinctions between "political Zionism" and "philanthropic humanitarianism."[106] "The ultimate solution of the Jewish problem must finally be sounded," he declared, "and the ultimate solution is the establishment of a Jewish Nation in Palestine."[107] With these words, Silver not only planted himself squarely in the militant Zionist camp, but publicly allied himself with Ben-Gurion and the dominant Mapai faction that controlled the Labor movement.[108]

Silver's speech electrified the conference and he won the enthusiastic support of the ZOA, Poalei Zion and Mizrahi. This unusual coalition, with Ben-Gurion and Silver at its helm, opposed minority efforts to whittle down Jewish claims to Palestine in order to appease the Arabs or Britain. Jewish immigration to Palestine, the coalition partners maintained in contrast to other Zionist groups, required neither Arab nor British consent. Despite political pressure from minority groups and some General Zionists and as well as the highly charged nature of wartime Jewish politics, the combative Zionist camp prevailed.[109] The conference adopted an eight-point resolution that came to be known as the Biltmore Program.[110]

105   Quoted in ibid., p. 777.
106   Quoted in Samuel Halperin, The Political World of American Zionism, reprint, Silver Springs, 1985, p. 222.
107   Quoted in Marc Lee Raphael, Abba Hillel Silver, p. 86.
108   Mitchell Cohen, Zion and State: Nation, Class and the Shaping of Modern Israel, Oxford/New York, 1987, p. 194.
109   Ben Halpern, The Idea of the Jewish State, second edition, Cambridge, Massachusetts, 1969, pp. 39–42.
110   Paul Mendes-Flohr and Jehuda Reinharz, eds., The Jew in the Modern World: A Documentary History, second edition, New York, 1995, p. 618.

American Zionism's organizational and philosophical differences notwithstanding, the Biltmore program epitomized the movement's progress since the Balfour Declaration of 1917. The political objective of establishing a "Jewish Commonwealth" became the common denominator and public demand of the major Zionist parties in the United States. This was a great advancement, in historic terms, over support for the Balfour Declaration's ambiguous promise to create a "national home for the Jewish people" in Palestine.[111]

Another characteristic feature of Silver's political leadership was his rejection of the elusive quest for American Jewish communal harmony. Nor, for that matter, did he promote Zionism as a panacea for all Jewish troubles. "No Zionist has claimed that the Jewish state in Palestine will remove all of the sufferings of the Jews," he declared. Rather, he argued, Zionism is "the solution for the national homelessness of the Jewish people which is to a large degree responsible for their recurrent persecutions and sufferings."[112]

Silver's qualified assessment of the Zionist idea illustrates his appreciation of Jewish life in the diaspora. At the same time, his lack of faith in the nations of the world highlights his conviction that Jewish survival hinged upon resolving the problem of Jewish "national homelessness." Against this backdrop, he viewed Jewish opponents of the Zionist enterprise with revulsion. For example, in January 1942 the philosopher Morris Raphael Cohen publicly attacked Zionism as "a false and near-sighted nationalistic philosophy" that raised unrealizable expectations among Jews worldwide.[113] In response to Raphael, who was then chairman of the American Jewish Committee's Institute on Peace and Post-War Problems, an angry Silver counseled his followers:

> It is in my mind important that we enter vigorously the arena of ideologic attack and defense. The desire for unity has blunted our weapons and our belligerency so that our opponents have now taken the offensive... Behind the suave surface pleas for Jewish unity in wartime, the forces of assimilation, the bitter enemies of Zionism are deploying for a major attack. They are again draping themselves in the flag of American patriotism, and they are hoping to make... all Zionists in America patriotic suspects. "Zionists are not Americans, only sojourners in America." This is dangerous business. I had thought at first that it would not be necessary to conduct a battle for Zionism among our own people, that we would be able to concentrate practically entirely upon the non-Jewish world. But clearly this is not the case.[114]

111   Ibid., p. 582.
112   Abba Hillel Silver to Emanuel Neumann, January 28, 1942. Wise Papers.
113   Morris Raphael Cohen, letter to the editor, New York Times, January 26, 1942, p. 14.
114   Abba Hillel Silver to Emanuel Neumann, January 28, 1942. Wise Papers.

Like other American Jewish leaders, until the summer of 1942 Silver believed that the Allies would not completely abandon European Jewry. However, the revelation of Nazi atrocities and the unprepared state of American Jewry convinced him of the desperate need to reinvigorate the central organizations of American Jewish life, particularly American Zionism. In the spring of 1943, Weizmann himself visited Silver in Cleveland in an effort to persuade him to enter the political fray. Weizmann's proposal ostensibly stemmed from his concern over the lackluster performance of the Emergency Committee for Zionist Affairs, which culminated in this period with the resignation of its key staff members. His suggestion, which was totally unauthorized, met with stiff opposition from the entrenched American Zionist leadership, notably Stephen S. Wise who wanted Israel Goldstein to become the next ZOA president.[115]

Finally, in the summer of 1943, a delegation led by Rabbi Irving Miller and Emanuel Neumann approached Silver and urged him to challenge Goldstein for the presidency of the ZOA. In reality, according to Neumann, Silver was disinterested in the ZOA presidency. However, he reluctantly agreed to be named a candidate as part of an overall plan devised by the Silverites. Neumann, Miller and others anticipated that Goldstein and Wise, who feared a public contest with Silver, would consent to appointing Silver co-chairman of the Emergency Committee in return for his withdrawal from the ZOA election. Silver approved the scheme and left the details to a negotiating team of Silverites. In the final stage of negotiations, however, he himself insisted on both the co-chairmanship of the Emergency Council as well as the chairmanship of the body's Executive Committee. Wise and Goldstein agreed to Silver's terms, and Goldstein was subsequently elected ZOA president.[116]

The political intrigue that led to Silver's appointment as co-chairman of the Emergency Committee solidified the animus between Wise and himself. Additionally, the individuals and factions that rallied around either man now developed into distinct political camps. Wise's supporters, known as the "moderates," favored a short-term strategy of attacking restrictions on Jewish immigration to Palestine. The Silverites, on the other hand, insisted on the primacy of the campaign for Jewish statehood. In this way, the conflict between Wise and Silver assumed national and seemingly existential proportions. It also had the effect of elevating the relatively inexperienced Silver to a position of chief responsibility, while humiliating an aging Stephen S. Wise and forcing him to limit his own authority. Wise thereafter

---

115 Emanuel Neumann, *In the Arena*, pp. 188–189.
116 Transcribed interview of Emanuel Neumann by Melvin I. Urofsky, July 1, 1975. P-515, Melvin I. Urofsky Papers, American Jewish Historical Society [hereafter Urofsky Papers].

complained to Nahum Goldmann, Weizmann's subordinate and the Jewish Agency's representative in the United States:

> I was perfectly willing to step out from the Chairmanship, but, although Silver could hardly bring himself to believe it, there are still people in and outside of the Zionist movement who, curiously enough, imagine that my name means something in American life. Neumann, I understand, spoke in insulting terms of me... I shall show my fellow-Zionists now that I am not to be shelved, I am not to be displaced, that I will exert my authority as the Chairman of the Emergency Committee, with Silver, of course, as cooperative Co-Chairman.[117]

Despite Wise's intentions, Silver assumed complete control of the Emergency Committee. As it happened, the timing of Silver's political ascension coincided with Bnai Brith president Henry Monsky's call for the convening of an American Jewish Assembly (later renamed the American Jewish Conference). Monsky proposed to unite American Jewry behind a platform for the rescue of European Jewry, the removal of restrictions on Jewish immigration to Palestine and the reconstruction of Jewish life in post-World War II Europe. After a lengthy process of propagandizing and balloting, the Conference emerged from relative obscurity to assume a position of prominence and public importance. In all, 501 delegates representing roughly 2,250,000 men and women from 64 national organizations and 375 communities comprised the democratic assembly.[118]

At the conference, there was unanimous agreement among the delegates concerning the rescue of European Jewry, the importance of postwar reconstruction and the restitution of minority political and civil rights in war torn Europe. The Palestine proposal, however, proved to be an issue of significant controversy. Indeed, in order to present a united front, a group of moderate Zionists led by Louis Lipsky, Nahum Goldmann and Meyer Weisgal had previously agreed to delete any references to "Jewish statehood" from the Conference proceedings. Not only was this agreement reached over Silver's strong objections, but the organizers denied Silver an assigned speaking position at the Conference.

When the Conference finally convened on Sunday evening, August 31, 1943, there was no assurance that the delegates would endorse the notion of an independent Jewish Commonwealth. At the opening proceedings Judge

---

117 Stephen S. Wise to Nahum Goldmann, August 4, 1943. Wise Papers.
118 *The American Jewish Conference: Its Organization and Proceedings of the First Session*, ed. Alexander S. Kohanski, New York, 1944, pp. 361–362, 373–377.

Joseph M. Proskauer, representing the American Jewish Committee, delivered a polemical address in which he declared that the battle for Jewish self-preservation "requires that we use every effort to avoid schism and achieve cooperation."

> We cannot all be Orthodox; we cannot all be Reform; we cannot all be Conservative; we cannot all be Zionists or non-Zionists or Revisionists. But what we can do is to take counsel together and work out for this emergency which confronts us a program to which all right-thinking Jews can adhere....
> My friends, we are in this Conference fellow-Jews and brethren. None of us is seeking to impose an intransigent will upon another. And while I have stressed the importance of unity of conduct, this unity must be built in the area of our agreements.[119]

Proskauer's address made the American Jewish Committee's position on the *Yishuv* a matter of public record. It would have been natural for a Zionist spokesperson to challenge this thinly veiled prescription for averting discussion of the ultimate political status of Palestine. On this occasion, however, Proskauer was followed by Wise, who sought to avoid conflict with the non-Zionist and anti-Zionist groups at all costs. "To act effectively is to act in unison," Wise explained. "Action in unison does not mean identity of thinking."

> Effective action is born of the capacity for adjustment in situations which call for agreement without compromise... I have not chosen to anticipate the program which only this Conference can adopt after the fullest consideration and fairest discussion... Whatever we may hope and plan is to be the future status of Palestine, and there may be room for discussion, its gates must not be closed.[120]

Proskauer's and Wise's addresses seemingly neutralized the discussion of Jewish political autonomy in Palestine. The next day, however, it became apparent that several Zionist factions — notably Labor,[121] Mizrahi[122] and the militant centrists[123] — feared an ambivalent Palestine resolution might be

119   *Conference Record*, August 30, 1943, p. 6. A180/69, Baruch Zuckerman Papers, CZA (hereafter Zuckerman Papers).
120   *Conference Record*, August 30, 1943, p. 5. Zuckerman Papers.
121   See the address by Baruch Zuckerman in *Conference Record*, August 31, 1943, p. 5. Zuckerman Papers.
122   See the address by Gedaliah Bublick in *Conference Record*, August 31, 1943, pp. 5–6. Zuckerman Papers.
123   See the address by Robert Szold to the Palestine Committee of the American Jewish Conference. Szold Papers; Emanuel Neumann, *In the Arena*, pp. 190–191.

adopted by the Conference in the name of communal unity. That the maximalist Zionist program was on the defensive was clear from the ensuing deliberations concerning "the rights of the Jewish people with specific reference to Palestine."[124] The scales were tipped on September 1 when Abba Hillel Silver gave an unexpected address during the general debate on Palestine. By all accounts, his forceful argument reversed the moderate trend of the Conference. His speech, an edited version of which follows, laid the groundwork for the final resolution on Palestine. "There is but one solution for national homelessness," Silver declared. "That is a national home!"

> Why has there arisen among us today this mortal fear of the term "Jewish Commonwealth".... Why are anti-Zionists or non-Zionists or neutrals — why are they determined to excise that phrase?... Why are they asking us on the plea of unity to surrender a basic political concept which was so much a part of the whole pattern of the Balfour Declaration?... We are told that our insistence on this Jewish Commonwealth is an insistence on an ideology, and why should one create disunity in the ranks of American Israel over an ideology?... We are not insisting on ideologies; we are insisting on the faithful fulfillment of obligations internationally assumed towards our people.... The reconstitution of the Jewish people as a nation in its homeland is not a playful political conceit of ours, a sort of intellectual thing of ours calculated to satisfy some national vanity of ours. It is the cry of despair of a people driven to the wall, fighting for its very life.... Are we going to take counsel here of fear of what this one or that one might say, of how our actions are likely to be misinterpreted; or are we to take counsel of our inner moral convictions, of our faith, of our history, of our achievements, and go forward in faith to build and to heal?[125]

Asserting a central role for the Zionist enterprise in modern Jewish life, Silver argued the case for an immediate political solution based on wartime realities. His moral position cut across ideological and philosophical lines, and the comprehensive Zionist program he placed before the Conference opened the floodgates of American Jewish consensus.[126] The Palestine vote was carried with only four dissenting votes. The delegates resoundingly called for "the fulfillment of the Balfour Declaration" and the reconstitution of Palestine as the Jewish Commonwealth. Next, the audience spontaneously "rose, applauded and sang 'Hatikvah' [The Hope]."[127]

124 Louis Lipsky, *Memoirs in Profile*, Philadelphia, 1975, p. 612.
125 Conference Record, September 1, 1943, pp. 4–5. Zuckerman Papers.
126 Samuel Halperin, *The Political World of American Zionism*, p. 234; Louis Lipsky, *Memoirs in Profile*, pp. 614–615.
127 *The American Jewish Conference*, p. 177.

Under Silver's impromptu leadership, the coalition of Labor, Mizrahi and the militant centrists prevailed upon the delegates to adopt an unequivocal Palestine resolution. The Conference accentuated the difference between the majority of American Jews who supported the total Zionist program, including the Labor enterprise in Palestine, and the small minority who opposed the mainstream. As for Silver, he carried the day not merely due to his inspirational address but because he articulated the emergent attitude of mainstream American Jews to Zionism. At the height of World War II, he supplanted Wise, Lipsky and others as American Zionism's preeminent leader.

V. From the Center to the Periphery

In the wake of the American Jewish Conference, Silver sought to transfer the mandate of the Palestine Resolution to the American Zionist movement. He started by changing the Emergency Committee's name to the American Zionist Emergency Council (AZEC). This switch heralded a new and forceful public relations campaign aimed at winning the American government's support for Jewish statehood in Palestine. He was joined in these efforts by Henry Monsky, Israel Goldstein, and Stephen S. Wise who were, respectively, the leaders of Bnai Brith, the ZOA, the American Jewish Congress, and the AZEC.

After 1943, the AZEC emerged as the main political instrument of American Jewry. For the duration of the war, Silver directed the AZEC's unremitting efforts to establish links with the American political establishment. He presided over a relatively efficient organization with an annual budget of approximately $500,000 that mobilized local and national support for the Zionist cause and the rescue of European Jewry through 14 professionally staffed departments, a bureau in Washington, D.C., a network of metropolitan councils, and a steady stream of educational, public relations, and propaganda materials. As a result, the AZEC developed into a highly effective "pressure group" and generated broad public support for Zionism. It also procured official declarations of support from thousands of non-Jewish organizations, hundreds of municipalities, scores of state legislatures, and a majority of American congressmen.[128]

Not all of these accomplishments, however, redounded to Silver's personal benefit. Between 1943 and 1945, Silver pushed the AZEC to embark on a series of controversial political initiatives and caused friction

---

128 Doreen Bierbrier, "The American Zionist Emergency Council: An Analysis of a Pressure Group," *American Jewish Historical Quarterly*, vol. LX, no. 1, September 1970, pp. 87–93.

with his old rivals. First, against the objections of Wise, he insisted on lobbying the United States Congress to pass a Palestine resolution favoring Jewish statehood and calling for rescission of the White Paper. Silver claimed to have enough support for the resolution, which he called "the most effective, perhaps the only way" to break the American government's "official silence" and place Zionism "on the national and international agenda."[129] Before its reintroduction and ultimate passage in December 1945, the resolution was initially killed in a Congressional committee by the lobbying efforts of War Department officials and Zionist "moderates" who wished to downplay the issue during the election year of 1944.

Angered by the sabotage of his political strategy, Silver used his leverage to ensure that pro-Zionist planks were adopted by the Democratic and Republican parties at their presidential conventions. This episode demonstrated Silver's ability to out-maneuver his political adversaries and force the hand of the Zionists "moderates." In addition to being a personal defeat for Wise, it was also a great embarrassment, for Wise was both a staunch Democrat and close friend of Franklin D. Roosevelt.

Though Silver's determined and aggressive tactics underlay much of American Zionism's success, in the end his seemingly non-partisan approach, which required the Democrats and the Republicans to court American Jewry's nationalist sympathies, caused an almost irreparable split in the movement. To be sure, the situation was exacerbated by Stephen S. Wise, Nahum Goldmann and other detractors who did what they could to stymie and, in several instances, undermine Silver's political efforts.[130]

The conflict between the Silver "activists" and the Wise-Goldmann "moderates" reached its zenith in August 1944 when Silver dramatically resigned from the AZEC. As the Brandeis group had done two decades earlier, the Silverites followed the example of their leader and resigned en masse. Unlike the Brandeis group, they had no intention of quietly pursuing their agenda from the sidelines. Instead, they established the American Zionist Policy Committee (AZPC), a quasi-official agency whose primary objective was to generate public sympathy for Silver. Led by Emanuel Neumann, the AZPC conducted a massive publicity campaign designed to foster the impression that American Jewry reacted with outrage to the "purge" of Silver from the AZEC.[131] "The Zionist masses," the AZPC asserted, "raised their voices in angry protest against the perpetrators of this destructive act, and made their wishes unmistakably clear in resolutions,

---

129 Quoted in Harold P. Manson, "Abba Hillel Silver," p. 15.
130 Melvin I. Urofsky, "Rifts in the Movement," pp. 195–211; Harold P. Manson, "Abba Hillel Silver," p. 17.
131 Marc Lee Raphael, *Abba Hillel Silver*, pp. 130–131.

telegrams and letters — all of them supporting Dr. Silver's position and assailing his opponents."[132] Most important of all, the AZPC won the unqualified support of the Yiddish press which published a steady stream of articles and editorials favoring the Silverites. "I don't know whether or not Dr. Silver has broken discipline," wrote a contributor to *Der morgen zhornal* [Jewish Morning Journal], an influential paper with a readership of nearly 100,000.[133]

> I only know that as Co-Chairman of the [AZEC] he took the only position which a Zionist leader can and must take in the present tragic hour for the Jewish people. This is not a time for "*shtadlanut*" [intercession] or subservience to the powers that be. Only an aggressive Zionist policy may be victorious. We have been overfed with promises. For over five years the White Paper [of 1939] has been hanging like a sword over our necks. During this period the enemy has drawn off a third of our blood. And what have our good friends in Washington and London done to make the future easier for us? In the fight against the White Paper they put obstacles in our path. What are we depending on? What are we waiting for? We — the well-fed Jews of America — can wait. But what of Hitler's victims...? An hour's procrastination may mean the loss of a thousand Jewish lives. How could a Zionist leader take even the smallest step to permit the Palestine Resolution to be killed?... The crisis in American Zionism can and must end with a victory for aggressive Zionism and its spokesmen.[134]

The AZPC campaign successfully bolstered Silver's political position. Upon his return to the AZEC he moved swiftly to consolidate his power base which included Labor and Mizrahi.[135] From this point on, Wise, Goldmann and others could do little to prevent Silver from asserting full control of American Zionism's political agenda.[136] In 1945 a reinvigorated Silver appeared unstoppable; he was elected president of the ZOA and president of the Central Conference of American Rabbis.

At this historic juncture, with Silver poised to reassert his leadership on the American scene, world events took a dramatic turn and the nature of Zionist politics radically changed. Roosevelt was dead and Harry S. Truman

---

132 *Public Opinion on the Zionist Controversy*, New York, 1945, p. 2.

133 Translated in ibid., p. 4.

134 Ibid.

135 Zvi Ganin, "Activism Versus Moderation: The Conflict Between Abba Hillel Silver and Stephen S. Wise During the 1940s," *Studies in Zionism*, vol. 5, no. 1, Spring 1984, pp. 73–83; Abba Hillel Silver to Stephen S. Wise, March 26, 1945. Wise Papers; see also *Independent Jewish Press Service*, December 29, 1944.

136 Albert K. Epstein to Abba Hillel Silver, April 21, 1947. Wise Papers.

was president; Nazi Germany surrendered and the destruction of European Jewry was public knowledge; the United Nations convened in San Francisco and the future of Palestine became a matter of international debate. Silver, who now enjoyed the overwhelming support of the American Jewish public, marshaled his resources to press for the Truman Administration's full support of Zionist demands.[137] Silver was unapologetic and forceful in his dealings with the president, and Truman resented the Zionist leader's abrasive style.[138]

While the Palestine question was only a "peripheral issue" for the Truman Administration, the question of American support was paramount for the Zionist enterprise.[139] Silver's political usefulness in this regard was readily apparent to David Ben-Gurion and the dominant Labor movement in Palestine. With his keen understanding of the American scene and global *Realpolitik*, Ben-Gurion sought to engage Silver's energies in support of the *Yishuv*'s political agenda. Silver, on the other hand, recognized in Labor Palestine a political partner of inestimable importance and the architect of the infrastructure of the future Jewish state.[140] To this end, he was prepared to enter into an "unholy alliance" with Ben-Gurion.[141]

At the Twenty-second Zionist Congress, held in Basel in December 1946, Silver and Ben-Gurion headed a maximalist coalition comprised of militant General Zionists and Labor. This faction, not unlike the moderate Zionist forces led by Chaim Weizmann and Stephen S. Wise, rejected the Morrison-Grady proposal, an American plan that called for the cantonization of Palestine. However, the Ben-Gurion-Silver coalition simultaneously opposed the Weizmann-Wise camp's willingness to participate in Britain's proposed Jewish-Arab conference in London. The London Conference, the militant leaders averred, would force the Zionist movement to capitulate to Arab demands and jeopardize future prospects for Jewish statehood. In the end, the Congress decided to withhold the Zionist Organization's participation from the London Conference but left open the possibility for the Zionist Executive to consider terms for the partition of Palestine into Jewish and

137   Abba Hillel Silver to Stephen S. Wise, September 14, 1946; Abba Hillel Silver to Stephen S. Wise, October (?) 1946. Wise Papers.

138   David McCullough, *Truman*, New York, 1992, pp. 598–599; Michael J. Cohen, *Truman and Israel*, Berkeley, 1990, pp. 65–67.

139   Jehuda Reinharz, *Zionism and the Great Powers: A Century of Foreign Policy*, New York, 1994, pp. 13–14.

140   See, e.g., Abba Hillel Silver to Stephen S. Wise, September 18, 1946; Eliahu Epstein to Abba Hillel Silver, June 27, 1947. Wise Papers; see also Zeev Tzahor, "The Histadrut: From Marginal Organization to 'State-in-the-Making,'" *Essential Papers on Zionism*, eds. Jehuda Reinharz and Anita Shapira, New York, 1996, pp. 473–508.

141   Transcribed interview of Eliahu Elath by Melvin I. Urofsky, June 5, 1975. Urofsky Papers.

Arab states. This decision, which signaled a turning point in British-Zionist relations,[142] placed Weizmann in an untenable political position. His credibility as the guardian of Anglo-Jewish cooperation was completely undermined, and he subsequently resigned the presidency of the WZO. Wise was similarly discredited and upon his return to the United States he resigned as vice president of the ZOA. In the end, it was not the new policy of the Twenty-second Zionist Congress, but the procedure for its implementation that made it impossible for Weizmann and Wise to continue in their positions of authority. This was precisely the objective shared by Ben-Gurion and Silver.

Silver reached the apex of his influence at the Basel Congress which elected him a member of the Zionist Executive, chairman of the WZO's political commission and chairman of the American section of the Jewish Agency.[143] In the ensuing year, though he fought with the Palestinian Zionist leadership over control of the WZO's political operations, he emerged as Labor's necessary diaspora partner.[144] He was also rumored to be a contender for the vacant position of WZO president.[145] Silver's final personal triumph came on May 8, 1947, when he delivered an impassioned speech to the United Nations General Assembly in support of an independent Jewish state.[146]

Following the creation of the State of Israel, Silver became entangled in the American-Israeli struggle for control of the Zionist Organization.[147] He subsequently resigned from his positions on the AZEC and the Jewish Agency executive. This time, however, he was not recalled by a mass of followers. Indeed, at the Twenty-third Zionist Congress in 1951 he and other diaspora Zionists were soundly defeated by the political machine of Israeli Prime Minister David Ben-Gurion. Silver's remaining years were devoted largely to Jewish scholarship, and participation in social and cultural work on behalf of the Zionist movement.[148]

Had Silver immigrated to the new State of Israel, he might have continued to play a central role in Zionist affairs. However, he chose to

---

142 Israel Kolatt, "The Zionist Movement and the Arabs," *Essential Papers on Zionism*, eds. Jehuda Reinharz and Anita Shapira, pp. 645–646.

143 "List of Members of Bodies Elected at Basle by the 22nd Zionist Congress (9–24 December 1946) and by the General Zionist Council (25–29 December 1946)," February 1947. A123/536, Emanuel Neumann Papers, Central Zionist Archives.

144 See Abba Hillel Silver to Stephen S. Wise, April 12, 1946. Wise Papers; Abba Eban, *Personal Witness: Israel Through My Eyes*, New York, 1992, pp. 94, 114, 117.

145 Marc Lee Raphael, *Abba Hillel Silver*, p. 154.

146 Ibid., p. 159.

147 See, e.g., "Ben-Gurion Warns Foreign Zionists," *New York Times*, November 7, 1949, pp. 1, 21; Abba Hillel Silver to Emanuel Neumann, August 25, 1950. Reel 49, Silver Papers.

148 Marc Lee Raphael, *Abba Hillel Silver*, ch. 7.

remain in the United States. Events quickly outpaced his authority as American Zionism's wartime tribune. Silver had been *the* maverick rabbinic leader in the United States. He was a Zionist in the then predominantly anti-Zionist Reform movement. He was an activist rabbi in a largely secular nationalist movement. He was a supporter of American Jewish bi-partisanship when most American Jews were still enchanted with the Democratic party. He was a leader who unhesitatingly — almost instinctively — bucked the Jewish and Zionist establishments at different points in his career. He diverged from American Jewry's elusive pursuit of consensus, known by the code words of communal "unity" and "harmony," and was willing to take calculated political risks. In the final analysis, however, it was not the American scene alone that determined Silver's rise and fall. As this essay argues, Silver's leadership was upheld and his strategy was implemented so long as his goals and those of the *Yishuv* leaders were congruent. After the State of Israel was established, a new American Jewish consensus took root and flourished. When this happened, Silver was swallowed up by the very revolution that had once propelled him to the fore of American Jewish life.

Contributors

RABBI ALEXANDER M. SCHINDLER. President Emeritus of the Union of American Hebrew Congregations. He presently serves as chairman of the North American Endowment for the Future of Reform Judaism; president of the Memorial Foundation for Jewish Culture; and vice president of the World Jewish Congress.

MICHAEL A. MEYER. Adolph S. Ochs Professor of Jewish History at the Cincinatti campus of Hebrew Union College-Jewish Institute of Religion; international president of the Leo Baeck Institute. His most recent project is editing and contributing to a four-volume history of the German Jews in Modern Times that is currently appearing in German, English, and Hebrew editions.

ANITA SHAPIRA. Ruben Merenfeld Professor for the Study of Zionism at Tel Aviv University. Among her many books and articles in the history of Zionism which focus mainly on social, intellectual and cultural history, her best known works are *Berl: the Biography of a Socialist Zionist*, 1985, also in Hebrew, German and Russian; *Land and Power*, 1992, also in Hebrew; and *Essential Papers in Zionism*, 1996, co-edited (with Jehuda Reinharz).

HASIA DINER. Paul S. and Sylvia Steinberg Professor of American Jewish History at New York University. She is the author of *In the Almost Promised Land: American Jews and Blacks, 1915-1935* and *A Time for Gathering: The Second Migration* which is the second volume in the Johns Hopkins University Press series, *The Jewish People in America*.

ARTHUR ARYEH GOREN. Russell Knapp Professor of American Jewish History at Columbia University and Professor Emeritus of American History at the Hebrew University. He is presently completing a book entitled *Jewish Politics and Public Culture*.

MARK A. RAIDER. Assistant professor of modern Jewish history in the Department of Judaic Studies, State University of New York at Albany. His articles have appeared in *The Journal of Israeli History, American Jewish History, American Jewish Archives*, and *The Jews of Boston*, 1995, eds. Jonathan Sarna and Ellen Smith. He is completing a book on American Jews and the Zionist Movement.

Index